TALK TIME

A Treasure Chest of Children's Talks

by

R. Howarth

MOORLEY'S Print & Publishing

British Library Cataloguing in Publication Data.
A catalogue record for this book is available from the British Library.

ISBN 0 86071 497 7

MOORLEY'S Print & Publishing
23 Park Rd., Ilkeston, Derbys DE7 5DA
Tel/Fax: (0115) 932 0643

To

BRIAN

PREFACE

"My dear children, I write this to you
so that you will not sin" (1 John 2:1, NIV).

This book has been compiled from true stories and legends, adapted and used by the author, to present as children's stories in church services.

The children and young people of today are expected to become the church members of tomorrow, and if this book will help others to hold their interest, kindle their faith, or present a lasting lesson or moral, then it will have achieved its purpose.

Biblical references are from the Authorised Version unless otherwise stated.

Torquay,
England 1998

CONTENTS

1. New Year Resolutions

Our first story for the New Year is about "Resolutions." Do you know what a resolution is? Well it means to make a decision. Our story comes from China where, when New Year comes round, the boys (and their fathers too sometimes) make kites of rice paper, which they call the Kites of Good Resolutions.

They believe that when they have made their New Year resolutions, if their kites keep steady in the air - they will keep their resolutions steady too, but if the kite drops or fails - then their resolutions will fail too.

It is said that there was once a Chinese boy called Pao, who had been promised a camera by his parents if he could get to the top of his class at school. So far, he had not done very well and had only managed to move from the bottom of the class to second from the bottom.

Anyway, New Year came round and Pao made a resolution - to get to the top of the class and stay there. He knew all about the Kites of Good Resolutions, and had asked his father to make him one, because he thought the kite might help him.

So on New Year's Day off went Pao with his father to the city wall, where already many boys and men had gathered to try and fly their kites. They were all hoping their kites would fly high and stay up in the air because it would mean that their good resolutions had a pair of strong wings. They did not want the kites to wriggle or fall, otherwise their resolutions would not be kept very well.

At last, amid some excitement, Pao's kite went up into the air and as it soared higher and higher he watched breathlessly hoping it would stay high and steady. It was just then when all seemed to be going well, that a terrible thing happened, the string from Pao's kite got entangled with another boy's kite, and although the other boy managed to jerk his kite free, Pao's fell down to the ground.

Well, you can imagine how Pao felt as he looked at it lying on the ground, his Good Resolutions Kite helpless and flat. Even his Dad was vexed and disappointed, and of course Pao's thoughts of having a camera now seemed very far off.

It was then that Pao, brushing away his feelings, had an idea. "Why should I loose my camera because my kite did not stay up in the air," he said. "I am going to get to the top of the class without that silly old kite. What will stop me if I work hard"?

And sure enough, as the weeks and months went by, Pao really did seem to be doing better at school, his school reports were good, and up and up in the class he went.

Finally, Pao did get to the top of his class and stayed there, and his father could not understand it. "It is strange," his father said, "how well you have done when your Kite of Good Resolutions fell to the ground so quickly".

"Yes," said Pao, "but when my kite fell, my will flew up to fill the empty space in the sky."

So Pao got his camera, and in earning it he learned two great lessons; he learned that when you want anything you must not depend upon others but work for it alone. Secondly, he learned that it is not always as hard as it may seem to get or achieve what you want.

Well we too can learn those same lessons from the story of that Chinese boy; many times throughout this coming year our 'Kites', ideas and dreams will fall and fail but if we will but have the will to fill those empty spaces in our skies with work and determination, then in the end like Pao we shall achieve what we want, and our good New Year resolutions will be kept.

2. Giants

This is the time of the year when pantomimes are in full swing, and I expect all of you will have heard or read the story of "Jack and the Beanstalk" and perhaps some have even seen the pantomime. You will remember how, when Jack had climbed the beanstalk, he met that terrible giant. Do you believe in giants? No doubt many of you do, including some of the grown-ups, or they did once.

It is said that anyone who does not believe in giants, should visit the churchyard at Hathersage in Derbyshire, for there they will see a grave about ten feet long and on the tombstone it says, "Here lies buried Little John, the friend and Lieutenant of Robin Hood," so you see both of these men really did exist.

And of course, we are told about giants in the Bible. You will all remember the story of the most famous of Bible giants, who was of course Goliath, but there is another giant mentioned in the Bible, in fact he is said to be the last of the giants. Do you know who he was?

He was King OG of BASHAN, and we can read about him in the chapter 3 of Deuteronomy - the story about him proves that he really was a giant. In verse 11, we read that the king had an iron bedstead that was 9 cubits by 4 cubits, and this works out to be some 4 metres long by 2 metres wide.

Now if a man needed a bed so large, then I am sure you will all agree - he must have been a giant. If we read about this giant king, we will see that he tried to stop the journey of the Children of Israel from the Red Sea, but he failed because God was on their side.

Most giants usually come to a unfortunate end, don't they? In the fairy story of Jack and the Beanstalk do you remember what happened? - Yes! Jack chopped down the beanstalk and the giant who was following him was killed, and we all remember how Goliath, that mighty soldier of the Philistine army was felled and killed with a stone from David's sling.

The lesson we can all learn from these stories of giants, is that although they exist in one form and another, and we are likely to meet types of giants in all walks of life, they will never beat us or really harm us if we do the things that are right and, like the boy David, show courage and have God on our side.

3. Sampson's Breakfast

You will remember that our last story was about giants, and there are many stories and legends told about these big strong men. In many parts of Britain, there are large stones or boulders which are said to have been thrown by giants, and our story today concerns such a stone.

Near the Scottish Highland town of CALLANDER, on the banks of the River TEITH in Perthshire, is a huge boulder which is perched perilously on the hillside above the Trossachs Road. It is known as "Sampson's Putting Stone".

This Sampson is said to have been the strongest man who ever lived, and a Scottish legend says that he lived with his mother in a hut on the slopes of nearby Ben Ledi. Being something of a strong youth, he naturally had a big appetite, so every morning, for breakfast, Sampson used to eat a great big bowl of porridge.

It is said that one morning, his mother started to prepare breakfast and then discovered that she had run out of oatmeal, so she could not give Sampson his usual bowl of porridge. Instead she gave him a meal of eggs and bacon.

After eating his breakfast, Sampson went for a walk to the top of the Ben wondering how he could pass the time away. Then he saw a boulder lying on the ground, and picking it up meant to throw it and hit Stirling Castle, which was some miles away.

However, Sampson had forgot one thing, can you guess what it was? Yes! He had not had his usual porridge for breakfast, and he was not therefore quite as strong as usual. Instead of a throw, his heave of the stone was more of a putt, as it left his hand it slowly trickled down the hill, until it finally came to rest where it now lies. It has been known since as Sampson's Stone.

The lesson from that story of Sampson is <u>not</u> that we should be sure to eat porridge for breakfast, <u>or</u> to think little of the value of eggs and bacon, <u>it is</u> that Sampson did not realise his strength.

Many times in life we fail because we too over-estimate our strength, we think that we, like Sampson, can move huge boulders, but we are not strong enough and the boulder only trickles away to remain still a burden or barrier to our lives.

How can we become strong when we are weak? - Well, there is a verse in the Bible that will give us the answer: Isaiah chapter 40, verse 31, reads - "Those who trust in the Lord for help will find their strength renewed. They will rise on wings like eagles; they will run and not get weary, they will walk and not grow weak".

Sampson failed because he was weak, so whatever our weakness may be in life, it is by trusting and serving God that we shall renew our strength, and become so strong that we shall have the power of an eagle or the strength of an athlete.

When we fail, let us remember not only the story of Sampson, but also how our strength can be renewed by serving God.

4. A Strange Stone

Do you remember what the last story was about? Yes, it was about Sampson and the stone which only trickled from his throw because he had not eaten porridge for breakfast, wasn't it?

Our story today is about another strange stone that is found sticking out of a pool of the River Spey, near BOAT-OF-GARTEN, also in Scotland.

It is said that many years ago, a certain woman of TULLOCH (a place on one side of the river) told her friends that when she died she wished to be buried in DUTHIL, which was on the other side of the river, and should the river be flooded at the time, if they took her body to the river bank, a safe way across would show itself.

Well, when she died, sure enough the river was flooded so her friends took her body down to the river bank as she had asked. Legend says that the waters of the river divided and left a path across the river bed, along which the funeral procession passed.

Years later, in 1865, to mark this strange miracle, a stone was erected at the river side and on it was an inscription which said that it was put there, "for a memorial of a signal of manifestation of the Divine power in dividing the water and causing a passage whereby the remains of a certain woman were carried over dry ground".

Since then, all kinds of stories and legends have been attached to that stone. Some thought the crossing was no miracle but a form of witchcraft. In 1867, the stone was found to be broken in pieces, yet no one knew how it had happened.

It is also said that a farmer who took away a piece of the stone and used it as a doorstep, later had his house haunted, and huge hailstones battered his house in the middle of summer, and stones fell from nowhere on the farmer and his family.

Well, we do not know if the story of the Stone of Spey or its legends are true or not, but it does remind me of a similar story in the Bible. Yes! The story of the Crossing of the Red Sea by the Children of Israel, which is told in Chapter 14 of the book of Exodus.

Like the old lady of Tulloch, the Children of Israel had faith, and even though they were encircled by the enemy with no means of escape, they felt that God would still help them - and He did.

Sometimes in our lives, it is only when we seem surrounded by the enemy, and all seems lost, and we do not know which way to turn, that as the strange stone of Spey recalls, there is a "signal of manifestation of the Divine power" of God, and He opens up to us a safe and sure way of escape.

When we find ourselves in circumstances similar to the Children of Israel, may we have the faith of the old Scottish lady of our story, and remember as the stories that both river crossings portray, that if we hold on, the power of God will be revealed to us.

5. The Boy Who Was Too Young

This story is a true one and comes from Canada, and is about a boy who had the will to work. His name is HENRY MAKOW, the eldest of three children, who was born in Switzerland in 1949, where his parents, who had been Polish refugees, met after the 2nd World War.

When Henry was two years old, his family emigrated to Canada, where his father, an electronic scientist, had got a research job. So young Henry grew up in his new surroundings in Canada, and when he was about 11 years old decided that outside his school hours and during his holidays he should be working.

He asked for work at a supermarket but they said he was too young, and he was told the same thing at a petrol-filling station and garage. Henry was so disappointed that he could not get a job that he decided that even though he was not old enough to work, he was old enough to be an expert on children, for after all he had been a child himself for years.

He decided that after being a boy for 11 years, he was quite qualified to write a newspaper column giving "advice to parents". So Henry sent a sample column article to the newspaper, "The Ottawa Journal," and when the editor received it, he was very impressed with what Henry had written and offered him £1 per week if he could write a column for his newspaper.

Within hours of Henry's first article being printed in that journal, a newspaper-man representing several papers flew from Toronto to see Henry and offer him a contract. When he was 13 years old, Henry's column appeared in 25 different newspapers and brought him in about £14 a week. Even some of the contents of his column were collected together to form a book called, "Ask Henry".

Well, the story of Henry gives us two great lessons, the first to grown-ups, that children are never too young to work and their eagerness must never be dismissed or frowned upon. Secondly, even though grown-ups may consider children too young, there are parts to be played in adult things provided there is the will, keenness and eagerness to work.

God chose many of His servants, not from men, but boys:-

David, a youngest son and while still a shepherd boy was chosen to be God's servant.

Moses, snatched from death as a baby, later became a great leader.

Samuel, when he was a boy helper to minister Eli in the Temple, heard God speak to him and call him to be a prophet.

Jesus used a boy who had a lunch of 5 barley loaves and 2 small fishes to perform one of His greatest miracles.

And girls too have been used by God. Do you remember the story of the little slave-girl in the house of Naaman, whom God used to help in the healing and leading of her master of God?

Even though Henry Makow was turned down in that supermarket and petrol-station, he fought back with determination and did perhaps greater things. You too may be turned down, or even consider yourself too young, but like God's young servants our own choice may not have been the right choice in His eyes.

Young or old, there is always a part for us to play in our Church and in our Christian lives - may we all in our enthusiasm be like Henry, and our works too be like his, and be read by all those round about and with whom we come into contact.

6. The Eight Sided House

No doubt a number of you like Geography at School, do you? I wonder if any of you can tell me where John O'Groats is? Yes, it is a little place right at the tip of Scotland and a favourite spot for tourists because it is the furthest point from Lands End in England, and the most northern point in Britain.

Our story today, is about the man whose name is given to this place. His real name was John de Groat, a Dutchman, who built his famous house at the tip of Scotland during the reign of King James the fourth. When he died, he was buried in the churchyard at CANISBAY, three miles from the house that still bears his name.

John ran a ferry boat to Orkney Island and charged four pence for each trip, and in those days there was a coin called a four-penny bit, which because of the ferry boat connection became known as a "groat".

It is said that John had seven descendants who were always quarrelling over who had precedence, or who was the greatest or most important. John solved the problem by building an octagonal house. How many sides has an octagon? Yes! It has eight, so his house had eight sides and eight doors. Even the table they used had eight sides so that no one occupied the important position at its head, and all were equal.

That story of how John O'Groats solved the question of who was the greatest, is somewhat similar to a story in the Bible. One day Jesus was asked by the mother of James and John if He would grant her a certain thing - that her two sons should sit one on the left side and one on the right side of Him in His Kingdom.

You can read about this strange request in Matthew 20, and of how the other disciples felt a little annoyed towards their two friends, who wanted this greatness.

But Jesus called them all together. Let's read what He told them in verses 26 and 27. He said:- "If one of you wants to be great, he must be the servant of the rest; and if one of you wants to be first, he must be your slave".

So we can all learn a lesson from John O'Groats and his eight sided house and his eight sided table - greatness is not measured by position or authority, but in being equal and in ministry and service to others.

If John O'Groats had built an ordinary house, he might never have been remembered, but his eight sided house reflected his thoughts for others, and so has made his name great.

Jesus was great because as He says in verse 28 of this chapter, He was to give His Life as a ransom for many.

We too can only become great when we give all for the benefit of others.

7. Puzzle Poster
(A Visual Blackboard Story)

If you were to visit the village of EAST HENDRED in Berkshire, outside the Plough Inn you will find a rather strangely worded notice board. This is the lettering that the notice board contains:-

"HERESTO PANDS PEN D ASOCI AL HOU R INHAR M (LES SMIRT) HA ND FUNLET FRIENDS HIPRE IGN BE JUSTAN DK INDAN DEVIL SPEAKOF NO NE"

As you can see, apart from just a few odd words, no one can read the notice, and no one seems to know why it was put there or by whom it was erected.

Each year, visitors stop and are puzzled by this strange notice board. Some have thought it to be written in a foreign Language, some have thought that it dosn't mean anything and is intended as a joke, just to make people stop and look at it.

On one occasion a minister in East Hendred was passing the Inn and heard a mother say to her daughter, "My dear, you know Latin, what does it mean?" But it is not written in Latin, and so the mystery continues, well - that is unless you know that there is a solution by changing the spaces between some of the letters so that they read as different words.

If I take a piece of coloured chalk and mark between the letters where a space is required like this:-

"HERE/STO P/AND/S PEN D/ A/SOCI AL/ HOU R/ IN/HAR M (LES S/MIRT) H/A ND/ FUN/LET/ FRIENDS HIP/RE IGN/ BE JUST/AN D/K IND/AN D/EVIL SPEAK/OF/NO NE"

Then you will see that we can now read that Notice and it says:-

"Here stop and spend a social hour in harmless mirth and fun. Let friendship reign, be just and kind and evil speak of none".

Perhaps it was a former owner of the inn who placed this inviting sign outside so that he would get more visitors, but even so there are lessons we can learn from this story of the Puzzle Poster.

Perhaps we are never understood, in our lives and actions, like that poster. Do others come to us for friendship and kindness? If they do, do they find those things? Are they written on our lives, or do our friends turn away because the good things about us are like those letters - in the wrong places, and we too are Puzzle Posters to them?

Perhaps like that poster, we too put spaces or barriers where none should be, and therefore we become misunderstood.

There is a lesson too in the words of that poster for everyone, - children, grown-ups, and the Church - if we individually and collectively, "let friendship reign, be just and kind, and evil speak of none," we should be displaying the greatest Christian poster or notice, that will lead others to read us rightly as true Christians and followers of Jesus.

8. The Two Doors

Many years ago, anyone who was a Christian and believed in Jesus, could be tortured, or put in prison, and even put to death because of their belief. Today, I want to tell you a legend about a Christian who was put in a very strange sort of prison because he believed in Jesus.

The prison cell in which he was placed had two doors, one door led to freedom, and the other to life-imprisonment. Each door was guarded by a soldier, one of whom always spoke the truth, and the other one always told lies.

The Christian was not told which door was which, or which soldier was the truth-teller, or which was the liar. Because he was a very good and sincere man, the Christian prisoner was permitted to ask one of the soldiers - but not both, one question in order that he might be able to choose the right door - the one which led to freedom. What question should he ask or whatever was he to do?

Well, the more he tried to think of a question that would lead him to be a free man, the more his mind became confused, and we can just imagine what he must have felt like. He did not want to spend his whole life in prison, he was a Christian - there was much work for him to do for Jesus and for others. It was then that he decided that as a Christian, he must pray that God would give him guidance, and so he knelt down in that prison cell and asked God to speak to him and tell him what to do.

Suddenly, as he prayed, an angel appeared before him and told him not to worry, and said that he should ask either of the soldiers this question, "Does the soldier who speaks the truth guard the door to freedom?" If he received "Yes" as an answer, then he must take the door guarded by that soldier. If he got the answer "No," then he should take the other door. Well, perhaps the angel's instructions need a little bit of thinking about, and this is something that you can take home and think about, but you can be sure that the Christian gained his freedom.

There is a great lesson for us all from this legend, and it is that whatever problems or difficulties we face in life, or however we seem to be imprisoned, the power of prayer can always help us to find the truth and lead us to the door of freedom.

9. The Man Who Reached Perfection

Perhaps some of the older boys and girls have done Biology at school, and like those who are preparing to be doctors, chemists, or dentists, have done some elementary dissection of small animals to learn more about their bodies or make-up, or anatomy as it is called.

But I wonder if any of you would cut up a lion in order to find our more about its body make-up? Well, our story today is about a young man, CHARLES LANDSEER, who did this in his search for perfection.

Charles, who was born on March 7th 1802, was not much of a scholar for books, but was encouraged by his father to go about into the lanes of the countryside around Hampstead, in London, to sketch any animals that he saw on his walks. When he was 6 years old, some of his nature drawings were so good that they were kept at the Natural History Museum in London, and a painting which he did at the age of ten, was some fifty years later valued at over eighty pounds.

When Charles was 24, he was made a member of the Royal Academy, the earliest age which is allowed, and he never stopped studying the subject of animals. That is why when he was 19 years old, he jumped at the opportunity of dissecting a dead lion, and what he learned from this proved of great value later on.

In 1859, he was asked to model four lions, and it was that early wearisome task but valuable training that helped him to produce the famous landmark of the four lions that sit at the base of Nelson's Column in Trafalgar Square in London.

Well, none of us are ever likely to cut up a lion, or even want to do so, but the story of Charles Landseer is a reminder to us all that if we want perfection, we must copy the original or study the pattern perfectly. To produce anything that is good and perfect, or worth doing or seeing, is the hallmark of a good artist or craftsman.

It is the same in our Christian lives, if we are to be true Christians, we must become Christ-like in all we are, and do, and say.

The Bible tells us that there is no one who is perfect, but we can all aim for perfection, and to become Christ like we must follow the pattern of Jesus.

Like the lions that Charles Landseer made, it is not so much the outline of ourselves or our lives that makes us Christians or like Jesus, it is the small details that make us a true copy or pattern of His Life.

To become perfect like Jesus, we like Charles Landseer can only reach perfection by hard work and dedication to our tasks.

10. The Coins That Did Not Sink

Have you ever seen a wishing well? There are many of these in various parts of the country and some are quite well known. In the model villages at Wimborne in Dorset, and Torquay in Devon, wishing wells have been provided as an added attraction. Some of these are constructed like proper wells and others like pools, and visitors are asked to throw coins in the wells and make a wish.

As you can imagine, even with small value coins thrown into the water, after a few weeks or months there is quite an amount of money.

Usually this money is taken out at intervals and given to a charity or some worthy cause, so people do not mind throwing in coins, and some believe that if they make a wish as they throw the coin - that wish will come true.

Our story today is about a wishing well many thousands of miles away, where the coins do not sink in the water. For over a hundred years, tourists visiting HAMURANA Springs, in New Zealand, have kept up an ancient tradition of throwing a coin into the pool.

Recently, a team of nine skin divers braved the ice-cold water of the spring and spent a day diving in turns to retrieve the coins, many of which were embedded in the rock and sand.

The pressure of water in the Spring prevents the coins from sinking and keeps them dancing about until they lodge in a crevice or on a sandy ledge. The divers brought over 10,000 to the surface, and the sum collected was given to the new technical school for mentally handicapped children in the nearby town of HAMILTON.

And so, even if the visitors' wishes do not come true, no doubt some wishes came true for the handicapped children's school.

Jesus once went to a well, not to throw coins in or even to wish, but no doubt to get a drink, and as He was there a woman of Samaria came to the well. She too did not go there to make a wish or throw a coin, but to collect water. Yet it was at that well that both received probably more than they could have wished for.

The woman gained more than riches: at that well she found the treasure of life. Jesus too was rewarded, for He found at that well one of

His greatest disciples, for the Bible tells us (in the Gospel of John, Chapter 4), that the woman went and told many in the city, and because of her, many Samaritans believed on Jesus.

People with problems and desires go to a wishing well and wish, but if we go with our problems to Jesus, we shall find there the Well of Life, because Jesus said, "He that cometh to me shall never thirst," and that memory verse will be more to every one of you than a mere wish.

11. The Silent Policeman

Our story today is about a Silent Policeman. Do you know what a Silent Policeman is? Well, I do not mean a policeman that does not talk, but something which does the same job as a policeman but without having a policeman there.

Well, no doubt some of you could perhaps think of several things, but what I have in mind is a Road Sign. A Road Sign is a silent policeman really isn't it? It tells people where to go, where they are, perhaps to go slow, when to be careful, and how far it is to a particular place.

Now let me ask you another question - which do you think would be the most important Road Sign of all? - Well no doubt you could think of a sign which tells of a dangerous bend, or a children's crossing, or something similar.

Perhaps one of the most important signs is, "Keep to the Left," because if the traffic did not keep to one side of the road there would be accidents all the time.

Jesus gave us a sign by the kind of the life He lived. If we were to follow that Road Sign, I think that we should find that it said, "Keep to the Right," and with three direction arms underneath.

The first one is, "Keep to the Right Thoughts," because it is so easy to be misled, and so easy isn't it to think evil if we don't get our own way, or if anything goes wrong.

The second arm says, "Keep to the Right Words." We often say things that we do not mean, or call people names, or develop thoughts which put unkind words into our mouths.

The third arm says, "Keep to the Right Deeds." I expect many of you sometimes do not want to go errands or give help when you are asked. Perhaps we sometimes pass by and pretend we have not seen people in distress. Or we do things behind people's backs when we should do good deeds willingly without needing praise.

Remember, the signpost that Jesus gave us points only to the right, and if we follow His signs and examples as we go on life's journey, we shall know when to take care, and when the road is open before us.

What a great destination there will be at the end of our journey if only we will follow the right signposts in life.

As you journey on, you will find many more signposts, which will have to be obeyed in order to stay on the right road.

Jesus gave us perhaps the greatest signpost of all when He said, "I am the Way," and He will help us along through life until we reach our destination. He will guide us, and keep us, and protect us, if only we will keep to the Right Thoughts, keep to the Right Words, and keep to the Right Deeds.

Whatever road or task there is in life, look for or ask if there is a sign to follow, there may be many, but only one will point to the right and that is the one to choose - it will be the perfect Silent Policeman.

12. The Mother Who Never Gave Up
(Mother's Day)

Today is Mother's Day, or Mothering Sunday, when we remember all the love and kindness which mothers have shown to their children and families during the past year. It is today that most children show their thanks by buying their mother a present, giving flowers or something else.

Mother's Day, as far as we know was first celebrated by the Greeks who called it "Mother Worship," and celebrated it in March.

In 1914, America made their Mother's Day official by their Congress fixing the date as the second Sunday in May, and they celebrate it with the children giving their mothers white carnations which is a symbol for the sweetness, purity, and endurance of mother's love.

In this country, we celebrate Mother's Day half-way through Lent which coincides with Spring and Spring flowers.

It is appropriate on Mother's Day that our story should be about a mother, and it is a true story about a Scottish mother who never gave up. It was during the 2nd World War that this mother was informed that the aeroplane which her son piloted, had been shot down over France and that he was missing and presumed killed.

The mother just did not somehow believe he was dead, although weeks and months passed and she heard nothing more of him. She was sure that he was alive, and so sure about it in fact that she carried on writing a letter to him every day just as she had done before, telling him all the local news.

Of course she could not send the letters, so they were daily added to the growing pile. I think if we had been in her position, and time had passed with no news - we would have given up hope and stopped writing letters.

But this Scottish mother didn't stop, the weeks went into months, and then a year passed - but she still continued to write every day. She had just finished her 400th letter when a most marvellous thing happened. What do you think it was? - Yes, her son came home!

You see, when his plane had been destroyed, he parachuted safely to the ground in France and had been hidden and looked after by friendly

French people, who managed to smuggle him out of the country to get back home.

Well, you can imagine the surprise that his mother must have got when he came home, and the pilot too got a surprise when he was given a bundle of 400 letters to read.

That story not only shows the faith and courage of that mother who never gave up hope, but it illustrates what most Mothers do for us all.

They never give up getting us our meals, doing the washing and mending. They never give up when housework needs doing or food and errands are required; they never give up when care and attention is needed when we are ill, or that something extra is needed for special occasions.

Perhaps we have taken all these things for granted in the past, so today on Mother's Day it is appropriate that we think what we can give up for mother - a little of our time, a little of our attention, a little of our help, or some small gift to make this one day in the year a real occasion that all mothers will remember.

13. The Boy Who Dropped a Light Bulb

Have you ever heard of THOMAS ALVA EDISON? Well, he was an American inventor who lived from 1847 to 1931. For more than fifty years he worked in his workshop/laboratory at MENIO Park in New Jersey, making all kinds of electric and telegraphic inventions.

Our story today, is not about Thomas Edison, but a boy called JIMMY PRICE, who worked for Edison, and about a day in their lives which brought great joy and sorrow.

It was about the year 1883, and Jimmy was about 15 at the time, and Edison after hundreds of experiments had finally made his first perfect electric light bulb. This was indeed a great day for Edison, to achieve something he had dreamed of for years. How proud he must have felt to complete a bulb.

He gave it to Jimmy to take upstairs, and a few seconds later there was the sound of a crash, and you can guess what had happened. Yes, the bulb had slipped through the boy's fingers and lay broken on the floor.

Well, what Thomas Edison must have thought to see that bulb on the floor in all those little pieces, after years of hard work and experiments. We can well imagine what we would have felt like, can't we? Yet Thomas Edison never said a word, instead he walked back to his workshop bench and began to make another bulb.

For days he worked until the new bulb was finished, and then Thomas Edison did a very great and wonderful thing. Can you guess what it was? He again handed Jimmy the bulb to carry upstairs. My goodness! He was taking a chance wasn't he? "Careful now," was all he said to Jimmy, and this time Jimmy made no mistake, he hung on and hugged that bulb for all he was worth, and this time he didn't drop it.

Well, that story has a wonderful lesson for us, in that Edison not only forgave Jimmy for his carelessness, but he also gave the boy another chance. I wonder if we would have done that had we been in his position? We may have forgiven, but would we after years of hard work have risked another accident and given another chance? - I doubt if we would.

Yet it was because of that forgiveness and trust that Edison put in Jimmy, that the boy made sure that he did not fail again.

Jesus was once asked by Peter how often one should forgive. Let us read about the incident in our Bibles. Find Matthew's Gospel Chapter 18 and verse 21.

Have you all got the place? Then let us read. Peter asks Jesus, "Lord, if my brother keeps on sinning against me, how many times do I have to forgive him? Seven times?" "No not seven times," said Jesus, "but seventy times seven." (GNB).

Many times in life, people shatter our dreams or seem to let us down, and if this happens to us again let us remember the story of Edison and the boy who dropped the bulb. Let us give those people another chance. Like Jimmy, they will be grateful we have not lost faith in them.

We too must also learn to forgive - not just once, but up to how many times? - Yes! Seventy times seven, which is 490 times if need be, which means we must do an awful lot of forgiving.

14. How The Robin Got its Red Breast
(A Story for Easter)

Our story today is only a legend, but a lovely one for Easter, and it is about how the Robin got its red breast. During the Life of Jesus, it is said that a little robin one day searched everywhere for food but could not find any - not even a scrap. And then, as it flew about the countryside still looking for food, it suddenly saw a great crowd of people sat listening to a man, who was talking to them.

The robin still saw no food about, and then suddenly the man in the middle of the crowd took 5 loaves and 2 small fishes from a little boy, and broke them in pieces, and began to pass the pieces round to the crowd.

Well, we all know of course this story about the feeding of the multitude, and how it ended in there being many baskets of crumbs collected after they had all had enough to eat. Well you can imagine that if there was all that food left over, the little robin found more than enough to eat afterwards from the ground where the crowd had sat.

Time passes, and our legend says that the same little robin was again one day searching for food on the outskirts of Jerusalem, when it saw a crowd and the usually quiet hillside was filled with noise. There was the noise of men shouting, and women crying, and hammer blows on nails. What was all the noise about? Flying to the branch of a tree, the little robin could now see what was happening.

The hillside was crowded with people, and they seemed to be gathered round three trees on the top of the hill. But the robin knew that there were no trees there, and saw instead that she had mistaken three big crosses for what she thought were trees, and on each hung a man.

The faces of two of the men were turned away from her, but the one in the centre was looking her way and she saw in His eyes not only great pain but also gentleness. And there was something else too about this man - yes! It was the man who had some time before fed that great crowd and left all those scraps of food when she was hungry.

The robin knew nothing about the nails or why they were hammered into the hands and feet of the men on the crosses. But she did see something she recognised on the head of the Man in the centre - there was a circle of plaited thorns on His head, and that drops of blood trickled from them.

The robin knew what thorns were, for only the year before she had built her nest in a thorn bush, and it had not always been possible to avoid the sharp points of the thorns as she had flown in and out of the nest, and she could well understand the look of pain on the face of the Man with the crown of thorns.

In a flash, she was perching on the bar of the cross - she knew how she could help, she hopped a little nearer and nearer, until she was close to the Man's head. Then she tugged hard at the largest thorn, but it did not seem to move, and then with her breast pressed against His forehead, she made a final effort and managed to pull out the thorn from the Man's head.

But as the thorn came out, a spurt of blood stained her breast a bright red, which has remained the colouring of the breast of all robins ever since - so now you know how the robin got its red breast.

Well, this story may not be true, but it does remind us once more of how Jesus died for each one of us. It is difficult for children and young people to understand the meaning of sin, and what was meant by Jesus dying on the Cross, but if we can remember the legendary story of the little robin and how it got its red breast, perhaps one day we shall understand better the Easter story of why Jesus died like He did for us all.

15. The Cabbage and the Mouse

Once upon a time, at a farmhouse in the country lived Farmer Jones, with his wife, their children Joan and John, a dog called Rover, a cat called Tim, and a little mouse.

Farmer Jones was famous because of the large and tasty cabbages that he grew. He supplied almost everyone in the neighbourhood including the King and his palace staff. One day, the king was to have a special dinner with may guests present, and so an extra large cabbage would be needed for the meal. The king offered Farmer Jones a large sum of money if he could provide the biggest cabbage ever seen in the country, complete with roots.

For days before the cabbage was required, Farmer Jones had been busy digging, hoeing, watering, and manuring round the large cabbages, especially one which seemed to grow bigger and bigger every day.

Apart from the cabbages, everything else on the farm did not seem to be quite so successful. The farmer was always checking their progress, while he in turn, was being checked by his wife for walking indoors with dirty boots. The children always seemed to be given jobs to do around the farm or errands to go - just when they wanted to play.

John was always teasing Joan, while she in turn always wanted the toys that John was playing with. The dog was always chasing the cat, which of course was always trying to catch the mouse.

At last, amid all the ups and downs of the family, the day came for getting the king's cabbage. Farmer Jones had selected the biggest one he could find and he dug and tugged to get it out of the ground - but it would not move. He called Mrs Jones to help, and she tugged while the farmer dug, but the cabbage still would not move.

Then the children came on the scene, so John and his Dad dug while Mother tugged, and then Joan helped with the tugging, but the cabbage seemed intent on staying in the ground.

Rover, hearing all the noise and commotion came along so John got him to scratch and dig with his paws round the roots, but there was still no movement, not even when Tim, the cat, joined the working party by helping to scratch round the roots.

Now all this time that the battle for the cabbage had been going on, another member of the farm family had been watching what was going on. Yes! It was the little mouse, and he too decided to join in. In and out he went of all the holes that the dog and cat had made, clearing the roots and fibres as he went.

Finally, with one big tug from all the Jones family, including the animals, the cabbage came out.

Well you can imagine how pleased and relieved they all were, and so the cabbage was duly taken to the palace, where the king rewarded Farmer Jones handsomely.

There are many lessons in that story for us all to take note of: It shows that the efforts of even the smallest can sometimes make all the difference and lighten the task of others.

Also, when we pull together as a team, unhappiness and differences are forgotten, team-spirit is cultivated, and things get done. When tasks seem impossible, let us remember the story of the Jones family, and work as a family to put things right.

16. The Strange Church Builder

Many years ago at the village of WINWICK, near Warrington, in Lancashire, it was decided to build a church. A site was carefully selected, the plans made and bricks and stones delivered to the site.

When the workmen arrived to begin building the church, it was found that there were two sites, because there was a big pile of bricks on one side of the road and a small pile on the other side.

They knew on which side of the road the Church was supposed to be built, but they could not understand why some of the bricks should be in a field on the opposite side of the road.

Anyway, the early stages of getting ready for building began, but every morning when the workmen arrived, they found that the number of bricks on the church site had got fewer, and yet the number in the field across the road had increased.

As you can imagine, this was something of a mystery. Whoever would want to move the bricks; and why? After a few more days the mystery increased as more and more bricks seemed to move overnight from one side of the road to the other.

At last, the builders decided to lay a trap and catch the culprit who was moving the bricks, and as nothing happened in the day, they provided someone to watch during the night.

The watch was made, and the hours of darkness began to tick away when suddenly the watchers heard a noise, it was something or someone approaching the pile of bricks. Then there was a noise among the bricks as if they were being moved, yet the watcher could not see any human forms, so they thought it must be some sort of animal. Suddenly as they swooped on the intruder they heard a series of loud grunts, and well - you can guess what it was. Yes! It was a pig!

For some strange reason, the pig had been carrying the bricks across the road, and some people when they heard who the culprit was felt that there must be a strange but good reason for this. It is said that some thought the pig objected to the bricks being put on his favourite land which was thick in mud - pigs like plenty of mud. It was also thought that across the road where the pig had carried the bricks was a better or drier site, while others thought that after what had happened there must be some sort of omen that the church was not meant to be built where it was planned, and so eventually the church was built across the road - thanks to the pig.

If you should ever visit Winwick Church, there in the boundary wall there is a carved stone plaque of the pig linking it with the building of the church.

There is a lesson in that story, just as God used that pig in a mysterious way in the building of that church, so He sometimes uses human beings. None of us are too young or too old to play a part in the building of His Church. We are not likely to erect bricks or stones, but we can all by our witness, and love, and kindness, and faith - like the Apostle Peter said - build a rock or foundation upon which the Church of God will grow.

When you are asked to do anything in the future to help your Church or perhaps your school, if you should think you are too young or too small to do very much, remember the pig, and what that small animal achieved for God.

17. The Mirror

There was a little boy called John, and next door to him lived a little girl called Joan, who unfortunately had spine trouble and had to lay on her back in bed all the time.

John was very fond of Joan, he felt sorry for her because she could not go out to play like him and other children, and he used to visit her every day when he came home from school, taking his toys for her to play with, or books for her to read. Every day he would tell Joan all about what had happened at school, or all the news that he thought might interest her.

One morning, a gentleman was out walking past Joan's house, and he saw a boy sat on the pavement with a mirror in his hand trying to catch the rays of the sun and reflect them onto a window. I suppose many of you have played with a mirror like that, and as you can guess, the boy was John.

The man saw that John did not seem to be exactly playing and it was the keen interest in what he was doing with the mirror that aroused the curiosity of the gentleman.

"Whatever are you trying to do"? he asked John. So John told him all about his friend Joan, and how as it was such a lovely sunny morning that he wanted her to see the beautiful sunshine, and he was reflecting the rays on her window to help to make her happy.

Wasn't that a kind act that John did? We too can be like him and that little mirror, because our lives are like mirrors - they can reflect good and bad. Next time the sun is shining, or even on a dull day, just say to yourself - can I be like John's mirror and bring happiness to someone else's life.

There is a childrens' hymn, one verse of which reads:-

Jesus wants me for a sunbeam,
to shine for Him each day,
In every way try to please Him,
at home, at school, at play.

Jesus once said, "Let your light so shine before men that they may see your good works".

Let us remember the story of John and his mirror, for Jesus also said that He was the Light of the World, and perhaps we too can reflect some of the Light to those in darkness round about us.

18. An Illness Made Him Great

In Toronto, Canada, lives a young man BARRY K. MACKAY, who in recent years has become one of his country's best known bird artists. He has held successful one-man shows of bird art, and has published a book on the rare birds which are found in the Great Lakes region.

Before living in Toronto, Barry had his home in Highland Creak, where he kept aviaries in which he had over 500 birds, and which attracted visitors from as far away as Mexico.

To produce a picture of a bird which can be sold, involves a long process: When he has decided which bird he wants to draw, he tries to obtain first a stuffed specimen of that bird. He has at least 1,000 different ones in his workroom, and he often goes to the Royal Ontario Museum in Toronto to see or borrow a specimen that he wants to paint.

Before he begins to paint a bird, he studies its habits, and what food it eats or other relevant points, in order that his paintings shall be true to life. Usually when he starts work at his drawing board, his pet sparrow-hawk ZIMA often perches on his head.

Well, as you can see, Barry Mackay is a very keen and thorough artist, but he may not have been a great painter but for having been ill. As a boy he was a very sickly child, and when he was 17 years old suffered an attack of inflammation of the brain.

Unable to take part in any games, he turned to sketching birds which he saw outside his bedroom window, and it was during his long struggle against illness that his home became a bird sanctuary to which people brought injured birds for nursing.

Barry's drawing of birds was still only a kind of hobby forced on him by his illness, but after a few years it was another setback that set him on the road to fame. His father disappeared leaving the family with no money and many bills that had to be paid, and it was then that Barry and his mother returned to Toronto, and he began to draw in earnest and then sell his pictures in order to raise money to support himself and his mother.

That story of Barry Mackay holds many lessons for each one of us as we think of his set-backs and no doubt many disappointments. When illness struck him, he could have resigned himself to being a permanent invalid and cut himself off from the world, but instead he found himself a new interest in the limited nature that he could see from his window. We very often give up when things do not go right, and we sometimes wonder why illness strikes - well let us remember the courage of Barry.

Illness made him great because he was thorough and exact in all he did, and this brought him perfection. If we are to be perfect in our work, and in our lives, we too must strive to get the small things right, copying only the right pattern.

There is a good text for us to read in the Bible, which is a fitting climax to this story. Matthew Chapter 5, Verse 48:- "Be perfect, therefore, as your heavenly Father is perfect" (NIV).

In our illness of heart, or weakness of spirit, let us remember to strive to follow the examples of Jesus. And if we do that in the little things as well as the great things as Barry Mackay did, then like him - we too shall become great through perfection.

19. The Tinker's Dream

At Swaffham in East Anglia, there once lived a tinker called John Chapman, who one night had a strange dream. He dreamt that if he went to London and walked along London Bridge, he would learn something that would be to his advantage.

The tinker was so influenced with his dream that he decided to go to London and see if it came true, so off he went. When he got to the capital, he made straight for London Bridge, and walked along the bridge - but nothing happened. He waited for some time standing on the bridge, and then decided that it must have been a silly sort of dream that he had, and that he had wasted his time, and his visit to London had been in vain.

Then he saw a passer-by, with whom he confided about his disappointment, who told John not to give the dream another thought because after all, everybody had a strange dream at sometime or other. For instance, the stranger told him, only the other day he had had a strange dream that in a place called Swaffham in Norfolk, there lived a man called John Chapman and in his garden was a tree under which was buried a pot of gold.

Well, John Chapman did not wait to hear any more, off he went quickly on his return journey home, and as you can guess as soon as he arrived back in Swaffham he started to dig under the tree in his garden. And sure enough he found a pot of gold, and then a second pot under the first, and in gratitude for his lucky find and wealth, he built the tower of Swaffham Church, which is still standing today.

We too, like John Chapman have dreams and visions, and sometimes we make wasted journeys in life, but sometimes God uses those wasted journeys to put us on the right path.

Like John Chapman, perhaps our greatest treasures lie round about us, but are unknown to us until we seek and find. There are three important factors in this story; firstly, after his dream John Chapman went forward in faith, secondly his faith was rewarded; and thirdly, in gratitude he remembered God. I am sure that there are lessons for all of us in that story.

20. Phoning God

No doubt many of you will have a telephone at home and you will know that every telephone has a number.

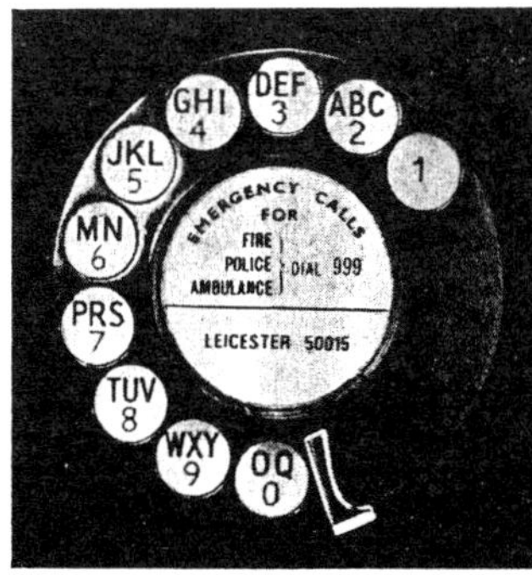

On most phones there used to be a dial with all the letters of the alphabet as well as numbers from nought to nine, and this system is now being re-introduced. As most of you know - to get the number you required you put your finger in the holes alongside the letters and figures required and turn the dial in the correct sequence so that your requirements were automatically registered through a telephone exchange.

In 1964, a Church at Dundee, Scotland, started a "Dial-a-Prayer" service, whereby a person could - after dialling Dundee 40333, hear at the other end a recorded prayer to give them comfort, and which was changed every day.

After this "Dial-a-Prayer" service had been in existence for some weeks, a Post Office engineer who had tried out the service, noticed something very strange when dialling the number 40333.

When he placed his finger against the figure "4" he saw that the corresponding letter was "G", for nought it was "O", and for "3" it was "D".

And so he was greatly impressed that when he was dialling the prayer service - he was also dialling "GOD" or really "GOD D.D" or as we say in arithmetic - God recurring, because the letter "D" is the abbreviation for God, (we use the letters D.V. meaning God willing or God permitting).

Yet there is no need to phone up God, because we can speak to Him anytime in our prayers and thoughts. Those prayers are more remarkable than a telephone with wires, for when we speak to God our thoughts and messages are sent to Him as though by wireless. And did you know that when we speak to God - there is something even more remarkable about our message - it is heard while we are still speaking.

Perhaps we have never thought before that God can be reached by all of us on this special phone He has made through Prayer, and He likes to hear from us all. In your times of trouble and difficulties, remember you can always get help from God by ringing Him on your special phone - you do not need to dial a number - just say His name and He will hear you.

21. Lucky Horseshoes

Our story today is about horseshoes which, as some of you know, are supposed to be lucky. Imitation horseshoes are given to a bride at a wedding to bring her luck in marriage, little miniature horseshoes are given to friends to bring them luck, while some people fix horseshoes over their door because they think their household will then be blessed with good luck.

Perhaps you may have wondered why horseshoes are supposed to be lucky. Well, the superstition arises from a legend concerning a saint who was called St. Dunstan, whose Feast Day is celebrated on May 19th, so our story today is about him, and how he came to be connected with the lucky horseshoe.

St. Dunstan was born near Glastonbury in the year 909, and it is said that he was related to the Royal Family of Wessex, and he had a good education. He may have had a very different career had not a dangerous illness turned him to become a monk, and it was as a man of God that he founded many Abbeys, which included Exeter, Malmesbury, Westminster and Bath.

He was principal adviser to all the Wessex Kings of his time and, in 959, was made Archbishop of Canterbury. He had many talents, he loved music and played the harp, he was a skilful scribe and draughtsman, and was also said to have been a bellfounder and a good metal-worker.

It is as a metal-worker, or skilled blacksmith, that he has a connection with our legendary story. One day, it is said that the Devil visited St. Dunstan and asked him to shoe his cloven hoofs so that he could get about better to do more evil. Perhaps some of you have seen a blacksmith shoe a horse? - Well St. Dunstan realised who the Devil was and why he wanted his hoofs to have shoes fitted, so he tied him to a wall and started making shoes.

He caused his customer so much pain however that the Devil asked for mercy, and St. Dunstan agreed to let him go on condition that he would never enter a place where a shoe for the hoof (or a horseshoe) was displayed. So now you know why the horseshoe is considered to be lucky, and from that story there is much that we can learn.

If we can keep the Devil not only out of our houses but out of our lives, then we too shall be lucky, in that no evil will befall us.

The Devil often seeks our help in assisting him to do more evil, and if we like St. Dunstan can only resist the temptation, and cause him pain by refusing to help in his evil ways - then he would think twice about pestering us again.

There is a story in the Bible, which some of the older ones will remember, told in the Book of Exodus, Chapter 12 about how the children of Israel escaped death because a sign was placed over their doors.

St. Dunstan was a man of God, and it is when we act like him as true children of God that we display a sign not only over our homes, but over our lives. That sign cannot be seen, but like a horseshoe, it will keep the Devil away.

22. The Blind Boy's Dream

In 1809, in the French town of COUPVRAY, near Paris, a little boy was born who was called Louis. We do not know much about his early childhood, but it was when he was three years old that he had a terrible accident, when in picking up a sharp-pointed awl or tool, it somehow pierced his eye and he lost his sight and became blind.

At the age of 10, Louis went to a special school for blind children, and it was while he was there that he dreamed of finding a way in which blind people like himself might be able to read.

Well, as you can imagine, without the use of one's eyes this seemed an impossible task, and yet he had several ideas but they did not seem to work out and he cast them aside.

It was when he was 15 years old, that he heard of an Army officer had thought of an idea of how his soldiers could read messages in the dark, and it was done by piercing a piece of cardboard from underneath so that the outline of the letters were raised on the surface.

Blind Louis knew at once this was the answer to his problem, and immediately he took an awl and a sheet of cardboard and for the next ten years tried and tried again to perfect a type of alphabet that could be done in this way for blind people to read.

It was after those ten years that this new language that he had made was called after his surname, and is today known to many thousands of blind people throughout the world as Braille.

Thousands of books including parts of the Bible and even the "Radio Times," have been published in this form of writing, so that blind people can now read as easily as you and I.

This story of Louis Braille surely teaches us all of a wonderful courage and persistency that he had, not only to help his own deficiency but to help his fellow blind friends. He knew that somewhere there was an answer to his problem, and he never gave up until he had found it - that is a lesson we can all learn.

Do we not sometimes give up after ten minutes when things do not seem to work out? Yet Louis spent ten years perfecting his dream.

We have our sight, but many times are blind to the things around us - the world of nature, the good things of life, and the thankfulness for our own sight.

It is strange when one thinks of how the very tool that blinded Louis Braille, the awl, became the means of punching that cardboard and giving a sense of sight to those who cannot see.

Maybe Louis was blind to the things around him, but he could plainly see a vision before him - that he made an ideal, and finally an achievement in the interest of his unknown friends. We too can think of that as a challenge to us all.

23. St. Elmo's Fire
(or The Man Who was Fed by a Raven)

Do you like thunder and lightning? It can be very frightening, can't it? There are many stories told to children as to what thunder and lightening really is. One class was once told at School that thunder was the noise caused by God moving forms about in Heaven!

Thunder really is the noise caused by the movement of the lightning and lightning is the discharge of electricity in the atmosphere or air.

Sometimes, if a storm is brewing or there is quite a lot of electricity in the air, one can see a bright glow often accompanied by a crackle appear at the top of ships masts at sea, or at the top of church steeples, and sometimes on the tips of aeroplane wings.

At sea on dark stormy nights, this glow is quite noticeable at the top of masts, or along the wireless aerials. Mediterranean sailors call it "St. Elmo's Fire" - our story today is about St. Elmo.

The name St. Elmo is a shortened version of St. ERASMUS, and his day is celebrated on June 2nd. Legend says that St. Erasmus was a Syrian Bishop who, when under persecution, fled to Mount Lebanon, where he lived alone and was fed by a raven. He was discovered, brought before the emperor, beaten with whips and clubs, and then rolled in pitch which was then set on fire.

As he remained unhurt, he was put in prison to starve to death, but it is said that an angel released him and took him to ILLYRICUM, where he led many to become Christians, even though he suffered many tortures.

Again an angel saved him and brought him to FORMIAE, where he finally died of his wounds. It is said that St. ERASMUS left behind a legacy to maintain a light which would burn around anyone who had faith or anything to give. He is the patron saint of sailors, and they regard "St. Elmo's Fire" on their masts as a sign of protection.

There are many lessons in this story about this Saint; because of his desire to be an effective Christian, he was twice rescued by an angel.

Escaping by running away from persecution, he must have wondered as he was alone on a mountain if he was doing the right thing, yet a raven fed him because there were greater things to be done for God.

Like St. Erasmus, we too may sometimes think we are being led away or failing as Christians, but as with him - God may have a purpose for each one of us. Even though our lives may seem insignificant and perhaps lost in the battle of life, God can use us as a beacon to others - as St. Elmo's Fire is to them at sea.

24. A Strange Zoo

No doubt most of you have visited a zoo, or at least seen one on television, or pictures of one. Most children like to visit a zoo because they contain such a large collection of animals, don't they?

Our story today is about what is probably the strangest zoo in the world, and it is in Jerusalem, where visitors tend to wander around with tit-bits in one hand and a Bible in the other.

But why a Bible you may ask? Well this strange Zoo in Jerusalem is what is known as, "The Bible Zoo," and do you know why? Well it is because all the different species of animals which are mentioned in the Bible except seven are to be found there.

The Zoo was formed by Professor SHARON SHULOV, who runs it as a hobby, and in all 85 animals mentioned in the Bible are to be seen there. There is something else strange too about the Bible Zoo because visitors find on each cage a little sign which gives the reference of the parts of the Bible where mention of the animal is found.

Now I said that there were 7 animals missing in the zoo which are mentioned in the Bible, and of these seven, four have never properly been identified, so it is not known really what they were.

The other three missing animals are the hippopotamus, the sabre antelope, and the oryx, and perhaps one day they may get these three to complete the zoo.

Well now, there is one animal in the Bible Zoo which visitors may think they have never seen mentioned in the Bible, but it is under another name, and I want us to read about it. We will find a long description of this animal if you will turn in your Bible to the book of Job, Chapter 42....

Now what do you think a Leviathan is? Well in that chapter of Job, the name is applied to a crocodile, but it is also mentioned in other parts of the Bible. Here in Hebrew the name means, "one that gathers itself together in folds," but it was originally the name given to a mythical sea-serpent or monster.

Well, I am sure we would all like to visit the Bible Zoo in Jerusalem; and perhaps the next time that you visit a zoo or pet store and see a crocodile, you will remember that in the Bible it is called a "leviathan".

And do you know who it was who gave all the animals their names? Well again the Bible will tell us. If you turn to the first book of the Bible, the book of Genesis, chapter 2, and verse 19, it says, "And out of the ground the Lord God formed every beast of the field, and every fowl of the air, and brought them to Adam to see what he would call them, and whatsoever Adam called every living creature, that was the name thereof".

Well, maybe now when we see animals in the future, we will not only remember that they are God's creatures, but remember too that it was Adam, the first man God made, who gave them all their names.

25. The Tree That Was Named After a Girl

Our story today comes from Japan and concerns a legend that has been told for generations among the AINU arborigines of HOKKAIDO in Japan.

The legend says that once upon a time, a beautiful Ainu girl called SEN lived in the village of PATUR-PI in HOKKAIDO, the northern most island in Japan. Sen's parents were very poor, and she had to work hard all day in the mountains helping to grow food and gather wood.

One day, a mountain demon, AKUMA, was struck by her charm and beauty - if only he could be like Sen with such beauty and delicate skin. So he followed her to the village, enticed her into a house, and then binding her with ropes, carried her to a mountain cave where he hoped he could learn the secret of Sen's charm.

You can imagine that in this rocky cave, Sen became filled with grief and cried all day and all night until her tears formed a small stream, which flowed right down the mountain to the village where she lived.

Now in the village, lived a friend of Sen's, a handsome courageous boy called YUKI. As Sen cried in the cave she thought of all the happy times she had with Yuki, how they used to gather nuts from the trees and play with them. Then suddenly, she had an idea - there were some nuts growing outside the cave, so she gathered some and threw them into the river of tears, and they were swept down towards the village.

Well, you can probably guess what happened - Yuki saw the nuts and this strange river and followed it to the cave. Here he rescued Sen from the demon, and the legend says that later the two got married and lived happily ever after.

But that is not the end of the story, the seeds from the nuts which Sen had thrown into the river of tears, grew into beautiful hardwood trees which were called after her. Today, Sen trees produce the beautiful Sen plywood, which is one of the biggest products of Hokkaido Island.

Well, no trees are likely to be named after any one of us, but there is a tree in Heaven on which we shall all one day depend.

It is called the Tree of Life, and the Bible says that it will bear fruit each month and its leaves shall be for the healing of the nations - this Tree of Life will be more remarkable than the Sen Tree of Japan.

26. Boy's Promise Saves Life

Some years ago, a woman in Scotland, lonely and desolate and afraid of the future decided to kill herself. She locked herself in the room of a Glasgow Hotel, closed the window, then turned on the gas and lay down to die.

As she lay listening to the hissing sound of the escaping gas, her eyes fell on a book that was resting on a bedside table - it was a Bible. She picked it up, and opened the pages, and her eyes fell on a verse in 1 Corinthians. Let us read the verse in Chapter 6 and parts of verses 19 and 20, it says, "Ye are not your own, for ye are bought with a price".

She then realised what she was doing, that it was not too late to start a new life, and so she rose from the bed, turned off the gas and opened the closed window. She did not realise it, but she owed her life to a boy who had kept a promise years before.

The boy was called, John Nicholson, who when he was 13 years old was given a Bible by his mother and she made him promise that he would never let a day go by without reading from it. Although he was so young, John faithfully kept his word even after his mother had died.

The years passed, with John still reading his daily portion from the Bible, and one night when he was travelling, he had to spend a night at a hotel, which was so full that he had to share a room with another man.

Would he remember his promise with another man sharing his room? Well John did, and with his guest looking on he took out his Bible and began to read it. No doubt he must have wondered what the other man was going to say, or perhaps what he thought of him, but John had quite a surprise - for his companion also took out a Bible and began to read, and he explained that he too read from the Bible every day.

It was from that chance meeting, that the two strangers decided to form a group of men that was later to be known as the Gideon Association, or The Gideons. They are a body of Christian business men, who have paid for, and placed more than 40 million Bibles in hotel rooms, Schools, Hospitals, and prisons all over the world.

John Nicholson, died at the age of 86. Because of a promise he kept, millions of men and women have come to know of the blessings of the Bible. It was a Gideon Bible placed in that Glasgow hotel room that gave that Scottish woman the will to live again, probably one of many who could tell a similar story.

There are many lessons in that story. One wonders if it was a chance meeting between John Nicholson and his companion, or was it arranged by God? John was not a minister or evangelist, but think of the work he started in spreading the Gospel to millions of people, and which is still going on today, and all because of a boy of 13 who kept a promise.

We can all follow in John Nicholson's footsteps by also making a promise - that we too will read from the Bible every day. And who knows - perhaps we too because of that promise may be the means of saving a life for the kingdom of Heaven.

27. How a Thistle Won a Battle

This is the time of the year when everything in the garden seems to be growing well, including the weeds. If you were to ask a gardener which weeds he dislikes most, there may be several answers but many would tell you a thistle, because of the many seeds it sends out, the depth of the roots, and how prickly it is to handle when pulling out.

Yet the world has not always had weeds and thistles, because when God formed the world there were no weeds or thistles, and do you know why they came? If we read the 3rd chapter of the first book in the Bible, called Genesis, verses 17 and 18, we will see that God sent weeds and thistles to make the ground more difficult for Adam to cultivate after Eve and himself had disobeyed God.

Now if you are ever speaking to anyone from Scotland, you must never call a thistle a weed, do you know why? - Yes: because the thistle is the emblem of Scotland, (like England's is the rose, and Ireland's is the shamrock, and the Welsh emblem is the leek), so you see no Scotsman likes his country's emblem referred to as a weed.

Our story today, is about a thistle and why it became the emblem of Scotland. It is said that over a thousand years ago, in the year 980 A.D., an army of soldiers from Denmark had landed in Scotland, and were trying to capture the main Scottish force so that Scotland would be theirs.

They found out where the Scottish soldiers were, and decided to attack them at night when they would be least expected. In order to make as little noise as possible, they were marching barefooted, but just as they were nearing the Scottish army lines, something happened! Can you guess what it was? - A Danish soldier stepped on a thistle with his bare foot in the dark.

Well, you can imagine how you would feel stepping barefooted on a thistle, and the soldier let out a yell, and his cry was heard by the Scottish soldiers, who guessed what was happening, and were able to warn their entire army. As a result, the Scottish soldiers defeated the Danish enemy, and it was then that the thistle was chosen as the emblem of Scotland, because the thistle had saved them from defeat.

And so it was not big brave soldiers who won this battle, it was a small useless little thistle, and so it is sometimes in the battle of life. You may feel small and useless, almost like a weed, of no value at all, but sometimes it is the little things which count the most and gain victories.

You too may be regarded as a weed by many because you are a Christian and attend Church and Sunday School, and perhaps because you are a Christian and an odd one out and fighting an army alone - you too become a thistle to others.

But like the thistle in our story, you will gain victory, because you will also be an emblem for God.

28. Heaven's Stamp on a Postcard from Hell

No doubt many of the older boys are stamp collectors, perhaps some of the girls too because stamp collecting is getting quite a popular hobby even with adults. Some philatelists, (as stamp collectors are called), not only collect stamps but post-marks as well.

I want to tell you today about Heaven's stamp on a postcard from Hell. Surely you are saying, "There are no postage stamps in Heaven," and as for postcards from Hell! - well now before you give up listening in disgust, may I tell you a short true story?

Some time ago, a Sheffield man received a postcard from Hell! He too, like all of us no doubt, had never dreamed or heard that such a place existed on earth, but sure enough it does. Hell is the name of a small village some fifty miles from DETROIT, MICHIGAN, in the county of Livingstone, in America.

The postage stamp on the postcard was of course American, and was one of a series showing Liberty, (the figure on the famous Statue of Liberty), holding aloft the torch of Freedom - perhaps some of you may have this series of stamps.

But no doubt you are beginning to wonder, "Where does Heaven's stamp come into it?" Well, on receiving the postcard, the man noticed that over the head of Liberty are the words, "In God we Trust". These words are almost an identical repeat of a verse in the Bible recorded in Psalm 18, verse 2. Let us read it together - "My God, my strength, in whom I will trust". Thus an impression or stamp from Heaven was on that postcard from Hell.

There is a lesson for all of us in this story. If we put our trust in God, we too like the Statue of Liberty, will be holding aloft a torch of freedom against any foe.

If we should be tempted by the devil, (with postcards from Hell), then by putting our trust in God, - we shall gain Heaven's stamp of victory.

29. The Clock that Strikes Thirteen

If you were to visit the Church of St. Marks at Worsley, near Manchester, you would find that the church steeple contains a clock which is very unusual. It looks just like any other clock, and you would not know that it was different from others unless you stood underneath it, or within distance of hearing the clock strike at 1 o'clock, and then you would find that instead of striking one, it strikes thirteen.

Well that clock has not always been on the church, it was only presented to St. Marks in 1946 for the church's centenary, (hundredth birthday) and our story today is about why the clock strikes thirteen at one o'clock.

Over 200 years ago, it was in the village of Worsley, that a local land-owner, Francis Egerton, who was the 3rd Duke of Bridgewater lived. In an attempt to carry coal from his coal-mines cheaper than by pack-horse, he commissioned the famous engineer, James Brindley, to build the first canal in England.

The canal was a great success, and led to many hundreds of miles of waterways that we have in this country today. And very soon the Duke of Bridgewater found that he had to build a boat-yard at Worsley, where the coal barges could be built and repaired.

You are probably wondering what all this has to do with the clock, well - it was when a boat-yard was built alongside the canal that a clock-tower was also included with just an ordinary clock in it.

It is said that one day in the year 1789, the Duke noticed some men who were employed in the boat-yard returning late for work after lunch, their starting time should have been just after 1pm.

On asking them why they were late, they told him that sometimes when the wind was perhaps stronger than on other days, or in a certain direction, they never heard the clock strike one o'clock.

Well, I expect you can guess what happened? - Yes! the wise old Duke thought up the idea to have the clock made to strike thirteen at one o'clock, and it has done so ever since even though the boat-yard has long since disappeared, and the clock has had one or two moves before its present resting place on St. Marks Church.

The Duke of Bridgewater was paying the workmen their wages, and expected them to give him their right amount of working time.

God has given us time according to our age - time for work, time for play, time for leisure, time for sleep and rest. Are we using that time wisely, devoting what we should to work and play, or are we trying to win time for our own desires?

Many times perhaps when you are playing and your parents want you to do something, a deed or errand, you think and perhaps say, "Oh! I haven't got time," because we do not like doing what we have been asked. Of course if one was asked to run a mile to a shop for some sweets or ice-cream, well no doubt you could all find time.

It is much the same with adults, those who work the hardest are often the ones who can find the time to help others.

So next time that you think to yourself, "I haven't got time," think about the story of the clock that strikes thirteen, and remember that other people - your parents, your friends, and God, have a right to some of your time.

If you set about the tasks that you are asked to do, and count thirteen like the clock striking, you will find that the job is half or perhaps done before the last count.

The old Duke of Bridgewater is long since dead, but his timepiece or special clock remains for everyone to see, and if you also spend your hours wisely, others too will gain from your given time.

30. Jigsaw Puzzles

Many children like to do jigsaw puzzles - do you? I expect some of you, particularly the older ones, have often tried to do them even if you have not always completed the picture.

Our story today is about a real type of jigsaw puzzle, and comes from Scotland. For about 700 years, a stone castle called Doon Castle had stood on an island in Loch Doon in Aryshire, and then in 1935 it was planned to build a dam in the loch so that a huge hydro-electric power station could be made.

As the dam would raise the level of the water 30 feet, the island and the castle would be covered with water, and so it seemed that this historic castle which had stood for so long would soon be seen no more.

Then someone had an idea - rather than lose the castle even though it was in ruins, it was decided that engineers would move it to a safe place on the bank of the loch. You are probably wondering however could anyone move a castle, especially from an island.

Well, first of all, every stone in the castle walls were numbered and the walls photographed from various angles. Then, one by one the stones, some of which weighed nearly a ton each, were pulled down and shipped to the shore of the loch, where the rebuilding of the castle began.

Using the photographs and numbers of the stones as a guide, the workmen rebuilt the walls of the castle, just as if they were doing a gigantic jigsaw puzzle. Well, I think you will agree that even though the workmen had pictures to help them, this was indeed a very hard jigsaw puzzle because all the pieces were huge heavy stones. As you can imagine, the work took a long time but finally the castle was rebuilt and stands today well above the water-level of the loch.

Life is very often like a jigsaw, we find ourselves with pieces and parts that don't seem to mean anything, or will not seem to join together. Very often we find that there is no real picture or pattern to follow, and we easily give up without our jigsaw being completed.

Many times, like Doon Castle, we seem to be alright and bearing a good position to the world around us, and then we find ourselves pulled apart and moved to new conditions and surroundings, and having to be re-assembled once more.

We may often think that we are too small to play a part in life's jigsaw, and we easily give up because we have no shape or pattern that seems to fit in with anything or anybody.

If we will keep the picture and pattern of the life of Jesus before us, He will help us to fit our lives together like jigsaw parts, which in the end like Doon Castle, will stand above the water-mark of all the waves and tides that try to submerge us.

31. The Monk Who Came Back to Life

Do you know what a monastery is? Yes, it is a kind of church where monks live, and perhaps some of you have visited one.

Our story today is about two monasteries that were built back-to-back at a town called SAN ANGELO; one monastery faced the main square while the other faced the hills that overlooked the town.

The monks who lived in these monasteries were very different groups, those who lived in the first monastery were very worldly and used to make wine which they sold to the local people. Those who lived in the second monastery kept themselves very much to themselves and were dedicated to silence.

In the first monastery, lived a monk called Brother JACOPO, a little man who was usually very quiet except for once a year when the annual fair came to the neighbouring town. He would visit the fair and always become heavily drunk with wine, and return to his monastery in the early hours of the morning singing at the top of his voice.

Well, this went on for many years and his brother monks did not like it because of the bad name it might give to them, and so one year they waited for him to return. When he came back, they led him down to the crypt or basement of the monastery, placed him in a hole they had prepared in the wall with bread and water, said prayers for him, and sealed up the wall with stones and left him there to die.

When Brother Jacopo came to his senses in the darkness, he realised what had happened and felt very sorry for himself, and his first thoughts were - could he escape from his death prison?

So he began to push against the wall. The newly sealed part stood firm but when he leaned against the inner wall it crumbled, and with a heave and a push - the monk found himself in the monastery crypt - but it was not his monastery, but the crypt of the monastery next door.

Well, Brother Jacopo, was so pleased to save his life that he decided to join the rival order of monks and live with them a life of silence. For a year, all went well, he never went outside the walls and he was satisfied with his good fortune, but when the fair returned once more he could not resist the temptation to visit it again.

Well, you can guess what happened, can't you? Yes! He got very drunk again, and in the early hours of the morning returned to his new monastery very happy and singing at the top of his voice, which wakened the rest of the monks.

Well once more, his fellow monks could not have this sort of thing going on, so again he was led to the crypt, put into a hole with bread and water and left to die. As the monks filled up the hole, Brother Jacopo was still singing at the top of his voice, and it so happened that at that very time one of his former fellow monks from the first monastery visited the crypt and heard his singing from the very spot where he had been sealed up in the wall exactly a year before.

Well, you can imagine the terror and fright that this monk had, and also his brethren when he went to fetch them, but eventually after thinking that what they heard could not possibly be true - they decided to knock the wall down. And when they did, there was Brother Jacopo very much alive with bread and water beside him and singing merrily.

His former fellow monks thought that this was such a miracle, and that he must be such a worthy man to survive like this, that they at once made him Abbot of the monastery.

Well, we can all smile at that story, and I don't suppose that Brother Jacopo ever told anyone the real truth, but his return to life is very much like an incident in the life of Jesus. When He died, He too was sealed in a tomb, but He came back to life so that the world might know His power.

We too are sometimes in our life's journey imprisoned or entombed through sin, but through the power of Jesus we can become free, and like Brother Jacopo not only have a new life, but become new creatures.

32. The Strange Light

Our story today is about a true incident that happened during the Second World War on the East Coast of England. It was during the war years that no one was allowed to show lights at night from doors or windows, and one had to use torches out of doors very carefully in the "blackout" hours as darkness was called, because if German aeroplanes were overhead - lights would have made them realise that they were over towns and they may have dropped bombs there.

One winter night in 1942, an English soldier was on guard on a lonely part of the East Coast near Leiston in Suffolk, when he saw a light on the beach. There were no inhabitants there and the beach was covered with mines and heavy barbed wire, so the soldier wondered at first if his eyes had been playing tricks in the dark and he had perhaps imagined he had seen a light.

But sure enough, there was a light there. Who could be on the beach at that time of night, and near the minefield?

The soldier began to wonder if the light had been dropped from an aeroplane to mark the coast for enemy bombers, or had an invasion party landed? Should he venture to find out? He was at first tempted to do this but his training told him what he must do - inform his guard commander, who immediately turned out the rest of the guard.

Everyone became very excited except the corporal of the guard, who remained very cool. He informed the duty officer and got a searchlight crew to stand by to light up the beach, and alerted the rest of the company.

Then he decided to find out what the light was, so carefully covering each other as they moved forward towards the beach, they crept and crawled alone by the minefield and through the barbed wire and all the time the light was still shining in the sand-dunes.

At last the patrol reached that strange light and what do you think it was? - it was a female glow-worm! To think that one tiny glow-worm could cause all that trouble, and the soldiers had quite a laugh about it afterwards, but it was not funny at the time, and they had at least done the right thing.

Now I said that it was a female glow-worm. Do you know why I know that? - Because it is only the female that really glows brightly in order to attract the male. And there is something else very strange about glow-worms, the female cannot fly but the male can, so the female sits in the hedgerows and lights herself up so that the flying male can see her.

Do you know how the female glow-worms turns on her light? Well, when she breathes deeply, hundreds of tiny tubes which are attached to her stomach fill with air. Around these tubes are millions of cells set in a substance which is called phosphorous and which glows when it comes into contact with the oxygen from the air, so the harder the glow-worm breathes and the brighter is the glow.

Well, our story today has taught you a little about one of nature's tiny insects, which one can sometimes see at nights in the hedgerows of the country, but there are lessons too in that story.

Even though in war-time everyone had to restrict the use of light (and were punished if thy didn't) that tiny glow-worm defied all the rules and regulations even if there was a War on, by shining herself. She was only a tiny glow-worm, but look at the trouble she caused by showing her light.

You also may only be small, but you to can shine. Yes, shine for Jesus, and even though wars may rage about you, there is a text in the Bible where Jesus tells us what to do - let us read it together in the Gospel of St. Luke, chapter 11, and verse 33, - "No-one lights a lamp and puts it in a place where it will be hidden, or under a bowl. Instead he puts it on its stand, so that those who come in may see the light" (NIV).

If we have a talent, or a light to shine even though darkness surrounds us, let us not hide it but remember the story of the glow-worm, and take a deep breath and shine!

33. A Lion Service

During the course of a year, there are many different kinds of services held in our churches such as Christmas, Easter, and Harvest. Also on New Year's Eve some churches hold a Watch Night service - where the congregation watch and wait for the New Year to come in.

Then there are Young people's services, Sportsmen's services, Pets services where the children take their pets along, a Plough service where a farmer's plough is taken to church to hope for a good crop and harvest from the ploughing of the fields.

But what is probably the strangest named service, and one you have never heard of before is a "Lion Service," which is held every year in the church of St.Katherine Cree, in London. You are probably wondering if lions are taken along to the Lion Service, well this is not so - but our story today is about how this strange service came about.

Over 200 years ago, there lived in London a man called Sir JOHN GAYER, and in 1646, he was Lord Mayor of London. When on his travels in Arabia, he was out one night with some friends. He got separated from them somehow and lost sight of his companions.

Suddenly he saw a shape coming towards him in the darkness. No doubt at first he thought it was one of his friends, then as the shape came nearer he saw it was the outline of an animal, yes! You have no doubt guessed what the animal was - a lion!

I expect that Sir John was very afraid when he realised what it was, and especially as it came nearer and nearer, but fortunately for him the lion passed by and he was safe.

Well, Sir John never forgot the wonderful escape that he had from the lion, and on his return to England he gave £200 to St Katherine Cree church, to be spent in a yearly thanksgiving service, and so this annual service has become known as the "Lion Service".

Well, perhaps none of us are ever likely to be confronted with a lion or have such a remarkable escape as Sir John, but in life we all have escapes from danger, sin, accidents, and illness, and we all have much to be thankful for.

We cannot all have special "Lion Services" in our churches to show our thankfulness, but we can all be as bold as lions when we go to church in thanking God for all the escapes we have had, and all the blessings we have received.

34. Bible Alphabet

No doubt most of the young people except the very young ones, can write or at least recite the letters of the Alphabet. Most know that there are 26 letters in the Alphabet starting with "A" and ending with "Z".

Did you know that there is a verse in the Bible that contains every letter of the Alphabet except one? I want all those with Bibles to look at the verse with me and help to find the missing letter. It is in the Old Testament in the Book of Ezra, Chapter 7, and Verse 21.

> *"And I even I ARTAXERXES, the king, do make a decree to all treasurers which are beyond the river, that whatsoever Ezra the priest, the scribe of the law of the God of Heaven, shall require of you, it be done speedily".*

Now let us go through the verse, and find the letters of the Alphabet to see which is missing:-

A is in **a**nd, **A**rt**a**xerxes, Ezr**a** etc.

B is in **b**eyond and scri**b**e.

C is in de**c**ree and s**c**ribe

D is in **d**ecree, **d**o, an**d** **d**one.

E is in **e**v**e**n, Artax**e**rx**e**s, d**e**cr**ee**, **E**zra etc.

F is in o**f**.

G is in Kin**g**, and **G**od.

H is in t**h**at, w**h**atsoever, **H**eaven etc.

I is in **I**.

J - ??? seems to be missing for the moment, so we continue:-

K is in **K**ing and ma**k**e.

L is in a**ll** and sha**ll**.

M is in **m**ake.

N is in Ki**n**g a**n**d do**n**e.

O is in G**o**d, and d**o**ne etc.

P is in **p**riest.

Q is in re**q**uire.

R is in A**r**taxe**r**xes, t**r**easu**r**e**r**s etc.

S is in **s**peedily, **s**hall and Artaxerxe**s**.

T is in **t**reasurers and Ar**t**axerxes etc.

U is in treasurers.

V is in river and heaven.

W is in which and whatsoever.

X is in Artaxerxes.

Y is in you.

Z is in Ezra.

And now you all know that there is a verse in the Bible containing every letter of the Alphabet except one, and that is the letter "J". Can you remember the verse? Ezra, Chapter 7, Verse 21.

There is some thing else about that verse that gives good advice to us all - Artaxerxes told the treasurers to do all that Ezra required of them, and to do it speedily because Ezra was acting and telling them what to do on behalf of God.

Sometimes, boys and girls, your parents and teachers at school and grown-ups, tell you to do things also on behalf of God, because God would also want you to do those things.

So like our Alphabet verse, when we are told to do things, we must do them in what way? - Yes! speedily - do it at once! because it is for others and not ourselves, and if we do that we shall be pleasing Jesus.

Now "J" is for the first letter of Jesus, and it was the letter "J" that was missing from our Bible Alphabet, so let us put our own "J" for Jesus in that verse by pleasing Him by doing all that is required of us, and doing it speedily.

35. An Experiment

If you were asked who was JOHN WALKER, you probably would not know or have a clue who he was - nor would the adults either.

Even when I tell you that he was a chemist and druggist who lived over a hundred years ago and had a small chemist's shop at STOCKTON-ON-TEES, in the north east of England, you would probably not guess why he was somewhat famous.

It was in 1827, that he carried out some strange experiments in his small chemist shop. He tipped the ends of three-inch splints of wood with a mixture of antimony sulphide and potassium chlorate (which are chemicals) together with starch and gum arabic.

When these splints of wood were drawn along a piece of sandpaper - it resulted in a smelly puff of fire, which set the piece of wood alight - yes! You have probably guessed that the first match had been made.

Soon these small pieces of wood were being sold in small boxes, each of which contained a strip of sandpaper on the side. It was some years later in 1852, that a grocer called Francis MAY, and William BRYANT, who was a soap and grease maker and sugar refiner, went into partnership and started England's first match factory at Bow in London.

Even today, the match still holds its own and is an accepted part of everyday needs for those who light pipes, fires, cigarettes, stoves, and of course for lighting birthday cake candles.

The firm of Bryant and May produced well over fifty thousand million matches a year - all because John Walker's experiment was successful over a century ago.

John Walker is not a well known person, and he never realised that the results of the experiment in his tiny chemist shop would produce a household article that millions use every day.

It is unlikely that we will conduct an experiment to produce anything that will have nation-wide fame, but we can all like John Walker in one way produce light that will help others who are in darkness.

Jesus tells his disciples not to let their lights be hidden under bowls, but to be put in candlesticks for all the world to see.

Our lights are not produced by sulphur or other chemicals, but by love, and kindness, and help to others. Like John Walker's matches, our lights are to shine before the face of all men that they may see and marvel at our good works. It is an experiment that may not bring fame, but it is an experiment that we can all try.

36. The Two Lighthouses

No doubt many of you have seen a lighthouse somewhere on the coast line, and know that they are placed in dangerous positions so that their flashing light can warn ships of dangerous rocks and ragged coastlines.

Our story today, is about a place on the coastline of Somerset called Burnham-on-Sea, which does not have a rocky coast - yet it has two lighthouses.

Although there are no rocks, there are other dangers because at Burnham-on-Sea a tidal river called the River PARRATT is used by cargo ships.

Now as this river comes in from the sea, it is called a tidal river because when the tide is high the river will be deep, and when the tide is low the river will be shallow and present dangers to ships.

One of the lighthouses is positioned inland, and the other one is set high on stilts on the sand. Their lights must be aligned, seen in a straight line with a ship's bow, if it is to enter the estuary of the river in safety.

So the captains of the ships position them so that when they look at the lighthouses - they see the lights one above the other and they know they are then in a straight line and on a safe course.

In life there are many tides which can easily carry us into danger, and often we too have to beware of situations like sandbanks and rocks which can be hazardous to us.

Often when we find ourselves in difficulties and troubles, we may have to look for a lighthouse to help us steer a course that will lead us to safety, otherwise we may be dashed against rocks or stranded in the estuary of life.

Jesus once said, "I am the Light of the World" - His life and example are a Lighthouse to us all, and if we should find ourselves in difficulties as we navigate our way through life, let us remember the two lighthouses at Burnham-on Sea and put our lives in line with that of Jesus - which will give us a safe course through the perils of life.

37. The Lost Ball

All children love ball games, and have played with a ball at some time or other, and no doubt lost their ball perhaps in the garden, or a hedge, or undergrowth, in the process.

Our story today is a true story about how a football was lost, and yet not lost, because its whereabouts were known.

It was in the village of TEMPSFORE, near Bedford, over 50 years ago when two brothers called JACK and KEN USHER, were playing football. During the game, Ken gave the ball such a hefty kick up in the air and on its way down it disappeared down a chimney.

Well, both Jack and Ken knew where the ball was - stuck down the chimney - yet it was no good to them there, so to the couple of brothers it was lost! After a time, the lost ball was forgotten and the two brothers grew into men.

In 1971, some 32 years after the football was lost, Jack, who was then 42 years old and a greengrocer, visited his old home in Tempsford village. He went to see the house where he had lived and found it being knocked down. While he was watching the demolition something rather strange happened.

As the workmen knocked down the chimney-stack, something came to light and you can guess what it was. Yes, it was the lost football after all those years. Well I don't suppose that Jack Usher was really interested in the football, but no doubt it brought back memories to him of all the many games he had with the ball and his brother years ago.

Many times in life we are apt to lose not only balls but articles, friends, and opportunities. It is when we find lost things we value them all the more.

The story of the lost football should encourage us to take care of all our possessions no matter what they are, balls or bicycles, books or toys. All that we have in the way of talents, intelligence, and our life itself, are gifts from God. Let us always treasure those gifts for if we lose them, we may not be quite so lucky as Jack Usher and find what we have lost.

38. A Seed is Sown

Many Christians often wonder what to do with old Bibles when they start falling to pieces and the pages begin to come out, or what to do with an old Bible when they have purchased a new one.

Because it is the Word of God, it does not seem appropriate to be burnt or destroyed. One old custom was for the owner of an old Bible to release each leaf or page to be carried off by the wind, in the hope that someone may find that page and read it.

Our story today is a true one about what happened when someone had scattered their old Bible pages to the wind. It was in 1914 when a young lady was given the chance to go to London to further her work. It meant her leaving home for the first time, and she rather dreaded the thought, so she decided to go for a walk to think things over before making her final decision.

While she was sitting on a seat in a park thinking over her problems, a page from a Bible fluttered along almost to her feet. She picked it up. It was a page from the Gospel of St. Matthew, and there near her thumb was the last verse of the Gospel (which is Chapter 28 and Verse 20) which seemed to catch her eye.

It says "Lo, I am with you always, even unto the ends of the world". When the young lady read it, it was almost as if it had answered her problems. She thought, why should she be afraid for the future, because whatever her future had in store, Jesus would be with her.

The young lady went to London to a new career and never regretted it, nor did she forget that page from the Bible which helped to make up her mind.

Sometimes in life like that young lady, a Bible text or a part of God's Word only comes alive and means anything when we read it in its true meaning. That Bible page gave an answer to the lady's problem, and if we will but seek through God's Word, we will find there is an answer to all our problems whatever they may be.

Wasn't it amazing how some unknown person by casting a Bible page to the wind could help that young lady. We would be in trouble for spreading litter if we did that today but, young or old, perhaps we can find a new use now for old Bibles. Surely that story should encourage us all to sow more seeds for Jesus, by passing on Christian books, or giving away our Sunday School leaflets.

Who knows, somewhere, sometime, a person like the one in our story may be searching for an answer to some problem, and the result of our sowing may not only provide that answer, but lead them to realize the power of God.

39. The Bible That Brought a Harvest

(A Story for Harvest)

Many years ago when Bibles were first introduced in the Pacific Islands, it was found that worms and insects seemed to take a liking to the adhesive which had been used in binding and gluing the pages together to form the book. As they ate the adhesive the pages became loose and the Bibles came apart. Someone thought of a good idea to stop this problem - cloves were used in the binding paste. Cloves are dried flower buds of a tropical tree used as a scented spice, and their strong smell discouraged the worms and insects from doing any further damage.

There are many strange stories told about the Bible, and today I want to tell you another true story about what happened to a Bible in Armenia, which is now a part of Turkey. The Bible was given to a man when he was a patient in hospital, and while he lay in bed he read from it and became very proud of his new book.

After he had got well and returned home, he told the priest in his village of how this book had been given to him and how from reading it he had gained strength. The priest asked to see the book, and when he saw it was a Bible, snatched it, and tearing it into pieces, threw them out of the window into the street. Even as a priest he didn't think ordinary poeople should have Bibles.

A grocer happened to be passing in the street at the time, and seeing all the pages picked them up and took them back to his shop, and later used them to wrap up small items which he sold.

Very soon all the pages were used up and his customers kept coming into the shop and asking for more of the wrapping-up paper pages. Almost everyone in the village had some of the pieces of paper or pages, and as they read them they all longed to know more of the wonderful stories that they had read on the pieces.

Some time later, a man came to the village selling Bibles, and to his amazement found that most of the villagers wanted to buy one, and he could not understand why his sales were so good until he was told the story. The seed of the Gospel had been sown in this strange way, and even though the priest had tried to destroy it, the good seed brought a rich harvest to the prepared hearts of those villagers.

Jesus once told a parable about seeds growing. Perhaps we could read it together as it is told in the Bible in the Gospel of Matthew, Chapter 13 and Verses 24 to 30.

The lesson for us from our story and the parable, is that we reap what we sow - tares or wheat. If we sow the fruiting seeds of trust, love, and kindness, even though enemies plant weeds, like the priest, they will in the end, bear fruit like those thrown away pages of the Bible, and bring a rich harvest.

40. The Girl on the Bridge

Our true story today is about a bridge in London, where on a bitterly cold night, more than a hundred years ago, a little girl who was poorly dressed and pale stood shivering and motionless as the busy London crowds hurried over the bridge to escape the cold winds on their way home.

No one seemed to take any notice of this poor little girl, until at long last one of the hurrying crowd paused and saw her - she was thin, and he noted that her hands were blue with cold, and her eyes seemed wide with bewilderment.

The stranger was a young Irish doctor, and approaching the girl on that London bridge, he asked her a very simple question, "What are you doing here?" The little girl gave rather a strange answer, "Waiting for God," she said. "But why here?" asked the man. "My Father is dead," said the girl, "and My Mother is dead too, but before she died she said that God would take care of me and I must wait for Him. I have waited a long time at home and He never came, so now I have come to look for Him."

The young doctor was moved to tears, and in a choking voice and taking her hand he said, "And you have found Him." Well, of course, the young man wasn't God, and he did not mean to be regarded as God, but in a way his words were true.

The young doctor took the little girl to his home and gave her food and warmth, and promised her comfort, and he kept his word, and in the years that followed he offered a home to many other little girls like the one he met that night.

If you have not already guessed who the young doctor was, he was Dr. THOMAS JOHN BARNARDO, the man who had started making homes for homeless boys, and it was from that chance meeting on that bridge that he started a home for girls as well as boys.

It is a simple story, and perhaps we may compare it with the story in the Bible of the Good Samaritan. On that London bridge a crowd passed that little girl but didn't see her, or if they did - they took no notice. But the Good Samaritan doctor came along, and not only took compassion on her but enlarged the work he had already begun.

There are two important lessons in that story. The first is that the little girl said she had waited for God but He didn't come, so she went to look for Him. We often expect God to come to us, and if He doesn't, let us remember the story of Dr. Barnardo's little stranger, and go and look for Him.

Secondly, we can easily be like the crowd on that London bridge, carried away and not thinking of anyone else. After all it was a bitter cold night. If only we could be like Dr. Barnardo and draw away from the crowd and see the need of the world around us as it really is, and show compassion.

We may never have the opportunity to start a great work like founding Dr. Barnardo's Homes, but like the doctor and the little girl, we might help others to find God.

41. A Lifeline

Helston, in Cornwall, is quite a famous town for its Floral Dance. Every year, in May, the inhabitants form a line of dancers and go in-and-out of the houses all down the main street. The town is perhaps less well known as the home of a man who became a life-saver.

Over 190 years ago, in Helston there lived a man called HENRY TRENGROUSE. In December, 1807, near his home on the Cornish coast he saw a ship-wreck. The ship was a frigate called the "ANSON" and 55 sailors of her crew were drowned during the wreck.

It must have been quite an experience for Henry Trengrouse to stand by and helplessly watch this wreck and see the cruel sea slowly destroy this ship and claim these gallant sailors' lives. There was nothing that could be done to help, except hope and pray that the winds and waves would moderate.

Henry Trengrouse stood on that perilous Cornish coast among the crowd who had gathered to watch. No doubt many of them had seen this sort of thing happen before. So near to land, and so much help near and available, and yet so little one seemed able to do. These were the thoughts that undoubtedly puzzled Henry's mind. As he thought more about it he vowed to try and do something to prevent these tragedies occurring.

If only the men could be pulled off the ship - but how could a rope be got to a ship in such a cruel sea. After months of thought and experiment, about a year later Henry invented the Rocket Life Line Apparatus which has since saved the lives of many sailors from ship-wrecks.

He was just one man in a crowd, one man of many crowds who had seen such tragedies happen - yet alone he did something about it and became a saver of lives.

There are many times in the lives of boys and girls, and grown-ups when we are one of a crowd and see the needs of the world go by.

Life holds many ship-wrecks for numerous people, and we have only to look around us to see these unfortunate people go down on the rocks of despair. It is when these events happen around us, that we should remember the story of Henry Trengrouse, and though we may be like him, one of a crowd, may we have the courage and initiative to throw out that line which may be a means of saving a life.

42. A Boy's Prayer

During the Life of Jesus, one day after He had stopped to pray to God, one of His disciples asked Jesus to teach them how to pray. We can read about the incident in the 11th chapter of Luke's Gospel, and of course you all know what Jesus told them to say - yes, it was the words of the Lord's Prayer.

Many people have composed their own special prayers, or have used verses from the Bible as prayers for various occasions. Many of our hymns were written as individual prayers.

One of the most famous prayers after the Lord's Prayer, is that known as "The Prayer of St. Francis," but it may surprise you to know there is "A Boy's Prayer". No one seems to have any idea of how it came to be written, or who wrote it, but we do know that some years ago the Rev. JOHN McGRIE recited the lines to his church at CAMELON, in Scotland, and they have been recited many times since as follows:-

A Boy's Prayer

O God, give me clean hands, clean words, and clean thoughts,
Help me to stand for the hard right against the easy wrong,
Save me from the habits that harm,
Teach me to work as hard and play as fair when I am alone,
as if the whole world were watching me,
Forgive me when I am unkind,
and help me to forgive those who are unkind to me,
Keep me ready to help others at some cost to myself,
Send me chances to do a little good each day,
and so grow more like Christ.

Amen.

Well, that is a wonderful prayer, not only for boys or even children - but for us all.

May that prayer be to you all a pattern for life just as the words of the Lord's Prayer were to the disciples of Jesus all those years ago, and to all his followers ever since.

Note to speaker: Have some copies of the prayer to give away if you think your listeners would appreciate it.

43. The Patroness of Young People

I expect most of you will know who the Patron Saint of England is. Yes! It is Saint George. Do you know the Patron Saint of Scotland? Yes! It is Saint Andrew.

But I wonder if any of you know who is the Patroness of Teachers and Young People? Yes! I did say Patroness, because this is a woman. Well it is Saint URSULA, and her feast day is celebrated on October 21st, but I don't suppose any of you knew this or who Saint Ursula was, so our story today concerns your own Patroness.

Legend says that Ursula was the daughter of a British king when the Saxons invaded England. She was sent by ship with eleven thousand other maidens to France to escape. On the voyage, there was a great storm and the ships were thrown off their course. Instead of getting to France, they reached the River Rhine, and sailed up to the German city of Cologne.

Now that Ursula and her companions were in a strange country, what would happen to them? It is said that God gave the answer by appearing to Ursula and saying, "Get into your boats and go on from here to Rome and ask the Pope to bless you, as great trials are ahead of you."

Ursula and her friends carried on up the River Rhine until they reached the Alps, from where thy continued on foot to Rome, where the Pope gave them his blessing.

They then decided to return to Cologne, but when they did so, they found it enveloped in fire and smoke. A savage and cruel pagan people, the Huns, had invaded the city, and it was too late for Ursula and her friends to turn back in their ships.

The Hun soldiers tried to make the girls their prisoners, but Ursula called out to her companions, "Be brave and resist! We shall belong to no one but Jesus Christ!"

The Huns set upon the girls and killed them with their spears, and it is said that a church was built over the graves of Ursula and her friends.

Well, you can understand why Ursula was made a Saint, and why she is the Patroness of Teachers and Young People - she was not only brave but showed tremendous courage and example to others.

Her final words to her friends, "We shall belong to no one but Jesus Christ!" are a worthy challenge not only to Teachers and Young People - but to us all.

44. The Marooned Sailor

In the town of LARGO, in Fifeshire, Scotland, you will find in one of the main streets, a statue of ALEXANDER SELKIRK, about whom I want to tell you our story today.

Alexander Selkirk, was born in Largo in 1676, and was the son of a local shoe-maker. Because of an unhappy love affair, he went away to become a sailor, and it was during one of his voyages that he was put ashore on the Pacific island of JUAN de FERNANDEZ, off the coast of CHILE in South America.

He stayed on the island for more than four years from 1704 to 1709, and one can imagine the adventures that he must have had, and having to find what food he could, and with no contact with the outside world.

In January 1709, Selkirk was rescued from his marooned ordeal by a Captain WOODES ROGERS with his ship "Duke", and he made Selkirk his mate and later gave him command of one of his prize ships called "The Increase".

In 1712, he returned to his home town of Largo, but he could not keep away from the sea and adventure, and five years later was at sea again. He died on December 12th, 1721, at the age of 45 while he was master's mate of "H.M.S. Weymouth".

Alexander Selkirk is not very well known outside his native Fifeshire, yet his adventures on that lonely island are known to boys and girls and grown-ups to all over the world - but how you may ask, seeing he was not well known?

Well, it was after his return to his home in Lower Largo, that he met a journalist called DANIEL DEFOE, who wrote a book based on the life of this Scottish sailor and the adventures he had on that island, and do you know what he called the book? - well perhaps some of the older children and adults have now guessed - it was "Robinson Crusoe".

I do not suppose that Alexander Selkirk ever imagined that his experiences and ordeals on that island, would later be read by thousands of boys and girls all over the world, and his story made into a film and re-enacted every year in Pantomime.

Our lives too, may be like that of Alexander Selkirk - just ordinary boys and girls and grown-ups, living a life that sometimes seems lonely in that no one seems to notice us very much. Sometimes our ordeals and problems are very much our own, and we may feel shut off and forgotten as though we too were on a desert island.

But like the writer, Daniel Defoe, who saw a wonderful story in this man's adventures, so too a writer in Heaven is writing about all our adventures, the ordeals, the hazards, and temptations, and noting if we too can overcome them.

Many times we may feel unknown like Alexander Selkirk, but if we become true adventurers and pioneers for God, our names may become like his, written as a famous 'Robinson Crusoe' in the Books of Heaven.

45. The Firework Saint

This is the time of the year when few children will need reminding of an event that happened many years ago, and which is officially celebrated on the fifth of November. Of course you all know it as "Bonfire Night".

No matter if you have a bonfire or not, most of you will know how this event came about. It is all because many years ago a man called Guy Fawkes tried to blow up the Houses of Parliament in London. But I wonder if any of you know that a firework is called after a famous Saint, and what that firework is? - Yes! It is a Catherine Wheel.

Our story today is about Saint Katherine, whose Saint's Day is celebrated on November 25th, and why the wheel is associated with her.

Saint Katherine, was born in Alexandra in Egypt. It is said that she came from a good family and was very clever and beautiful.

She was a Christian and she protested to the Emperor MAXENTIUS, against the worship of idols that he tried to enforce. The emperor asked Katherine to deny her faith and marry him, but she refused. The emperor had her imprisoned and beaten for two hours each day.

Legend says that her faith was strengthened because when she was in prison, a dove brought food to her cell, and that Jesus appeared to her in a vision.

A further attempt was made by the Emperor to break her faith down by threatening to kill her with a spiked or knifed wheel, (the Catherine Wheel), but it fell to pieces and she was unhurt, but many of the people who had come along to see her killed - were killed themselves by flying splinters from the wheel.

After the ordeal of the wheel, Katherine persuaded 200 soldiers to become Christians and they were at once beheaded. Finally as Katherine herself was beheaded she called down blessings from Heaven on all who should remember her.

It is said that after she had been killed, angels took her body to be buried on Mount Sinai, where a monastery was built to her name. (It was on Mount Sinai that Moses once saw a strange bonfire, which was made by God, and which you can read about in the Bible in the 24th Chapter of the Book of Exodus.)

Now you know why one of your fireworks is called a Catherine Wheel, and why it throws out sparks, similar to the first Katherine Wheel that threw out splinters.

Perhaps next time you see a Catherine wheel you will remember Saint Katherine and her faith, and remember too her courage of how she stood up against the emperor, and even as a woman, she could lead 200 soldiers to become Christians - she was indeed something of a firework herself!

46. A Strange Memorial

Usually monuments and memorials are erected to good men and women, or to someone who has done some noble deed, and this is the time of the year when we remember those who have died in the service of their country and poppy wreaths are placed on the many War Memorials.

Our story today, however, is about a memorial that was carved to villains. If you were to visit Brittany in France and walk the 3 or 4 miles along the coast from PAREME to the little village of ROTHENEUF, you would notice a sudden change in the coastline.

Instead of the sun drenched sands that extend beyond Pareme, you would find black cliffs and razor-sharp rocks that jut out of the treacherous sea.

At Rotheneuf, huge monstrous carvings have been made out of the rock face of mens heads that look terribly frightening. The heads are bare or wearing funny hats, and the faces seem to frown, or lear and grin at you wherever you turn.

You are probably wondering what these carvings are and how they came to be there; the village to Rotheneuf takes its name from a family who lived there in 17th century (300 years ago) and who were very evil and terrorized land and sea along the coast by their treachery.

They lured ships towards the coast, and then when they became wrecked on the sharp rocks, the Rotheneuf family robbed and plundered, and were guilty of murder and piracy among the wrecks.

After many years, a priest called L'ABBE FOURE went to the village, and he was so shocked by the crimes and evil of the pirate family that he spent 25 years of his life carving their likeness out of the granite rock face. These carvings are indeed a strange monument, and it was a strange task for a minister to do and spend 25 years doing it - yet there is something we can learn from those carvings.

The monument to the villains was erected so as to show up their bad deeds and as a warning to others. Perhaps we may consider the work of the priest over 25 years to have been a waste of time for a man of God, but if his work led others to see the folly of these pirates, and perhaps keep them on the right road, then his work was not done in vain.

Any good that the pirates may have done was forgotten or known only to a few, but their evil has remained for thousands to see over the years.

It is the same with our lives - our good deeds are rarely seen by others, but if we did anything bad or committed a crime - it would be in the newspapers and thousands who do not even know us would never-the-less read about us.

I said that our good deeds are rarely seen by others, but you know God sees them and records all that we do. So when we are tempted between good and bad, let us remember the story of those pirates in Brittany, and decide that it is better to have a monument of good in Heaven that a memorial of evil on Earth.

47. The Little Church

There is a house at Conway, in North Wales, which claims to be the smallest house in Great Britain, and I don't think this has ever been disputed. It attracts thousands of visitors every year.

There is however quite a lot of competition as to which is the smallest church in Great Britain, many have claimed this title and perhaps it will never be proved.

What has been proved however is that the smallest church in the world is in a place called MAINE, in America, and inside it measures only 7 feet one way by 4½ feet the other way, which is smaller than most small kitchens or bedrooms.

This small church is said to have just enough room for a minister and a congregation of two people, which is indeed very small, and goodness knows what would happen if any visitors went along to services.

Yet you know the greatness of a church or building, or even a person is not measured by size - it is what it is. It is not the massive Cathedral, or village church, or tiny mission hall, which is important, but the people inside and why they are there.

All churches would like to see more people at services, and all Sunday Schools would like to have more children in the classes, but it is not numbers or quantity that counts, but quality.

Jesus once told His disciples what He expected of churches and the number of people attending them. Let us read from the Gospel of Matthew Chapter 18 Verse 20, "For where two or three are gathered together in My Name, there am I in the midst of them".

So you see, the size of a church and the number of people is not important - it is why we are there and gathered in the name of Jesus to worship God. When we are really thankful for all the happiness and good things of life that come our way (and these blessings come every day of the week as well as Sunday) as long as two or more are gathered in the name of Jesus to thank and worship God - there is a church!

That means that a church can be made anywhere - on the high seas, in the desert, on mountain tops - wherever two or more want to give thanks and praise to God.

When we want to speak to God, let us all remember the story of the little church in America, and think that it is not so odd after all, because we create "a church" like that anytime and anywhere we like.

There is also a lesson for us all in what Jesus promised about where two or more were gathered in His Name - do you remember what it was? Yes! There He would be in the midst.

It is very difficult for children to accept that although we cannot see Jesus, He is there! But as you grow older you will learn more of this great mystery.

As we go through life, there will be many times when we need Jesus to help us, protect us, and lead us, and how do we get Him on our side? Yes! We make our own little church so that we are with Him and He is with us.

48. The Man Who Took an Evening Walk

In the Victoria Embankment Gardens in London, there is a statue of a man holding an open Bible in his hand as though inviting people to read it. He was not a minister, but he started one of the greatest Christian institutions ever - his name was ROBERT RAIKES.

It was on a dark evening in 1780, that Robert Raikes, a wealthy printer and editor in Gloucester, took a walk along Sooty Alley, a muddy street in the slum district of the town. As he walked along with a servant ahead of him with a lantern, quite a lot of dirty ragged children in the street shouted nasty remarks to him, and one hit him in the middle of his back with a handful of mud.

He went for shelter in a doorway, and when a woman came along to see what all the noise was about, Raikes told her that the parents of the children should feel ashamed of the way they acted. She said, "Yes sir, but the children work all day, and at night they have nowhere to go or play, and nothing to do, and you should see what it is like on Sundays."

Well, Raikes went back to visit Sooty Alley the next Sunday afternoon, and what he saw appalled him, older boys were swearing and fighting, and setting younger boys against each other with others watching or rolling about on the muddy ground.

Many of these children worked in factories and workshops at six years of age, most of them working 12 hours a day. Eight out of ten boys were in prison before they were 21, and one in four usually finished up with such crimes that they were hanged.

Robert Raikes, was the leader of a group of people who sent aid to those in prisons, and he was proud to be known as, "the man who helps the poor". On that Sunday afternoon he realised that it would take more than gifts of money to help those children - they needed something to do on Sundays - the one day of the week when they were allowed to be idle.

Raikes was a very keen churchman, and he decided that the children should be brought together for some kind of religious teaching, and he was able to get the help of Mrs King of St. Catherine Street.

He won the consent of parents, and by offering sweets and pennies, he rounded up a dozen boys one Sunday morning and led them to Mrs

King's house, where he read them parts of the Bible and told them stories with simple morals.

Sunday by Sunday, the crowd of ragged children grew as word began to spread around that there were sweets and pennies to be had if they went to Mrs King's house and sat still and listened, and very soon girls as well as boys begged to be allowed to attend.

And so every Sunday morning, the tall Robert Raikes dressed in his velvet coat and silver-buckled shoes was to be seen leading a crowd of rowdy children down St. Catherine Street in Gloucester to what was becoming known as, "Raike's Sabbath School," but which others called, "Raike's Ragged School".

It was from the Ragged School, that there developed the modern Sunday School, an institution that now covers the world. Today millions of young people and adults regularly receive religious instruction in churches of almost every creed from voluntary teachers in these schools - which is probably the mightiest force on earth for moral training and character-building outside the home.

Before Robert Raikes died at the age of 75 in 1811, he saw the hours of labour shortened for children at work so that they might attend school. Later the Sunday School Union, formed in 1803, helped to bring about the Education Act of 1870, which compelled local authorities to provide day schools for all children in the British Isles.

The World Council of Christian Education estimated that in 1960, there was a total Protestant Sunday School membership of at least 64 million children. And so the influence of Robert Raike's Ragged School grows. He once wrote, "Perhaps what we have started will some day far exceed our first expectations."

Those words could well be a challenge to us all, and when we perhaps think of humble beginnings in life, let us remember the mighty work that began because Robert Raikes took an evening walk in that poor district of Gloucester.

49. A Nursing Heroine

In the history of our country, there have been men who have been proclaimed a hero because of their courage or loyalty, and although perhaps in comparison not many women have become national heroines - our story today is about such a person.

It is appropriate that we remember her today because she was born on December 4th 1865, in the village of SWARDESTON, in Norfolk, and her name was EDITH CAVELL.

At the age of 30, she went to a London hospital to become a nurse, and gained promotions until she became an assistant matron.

In 1907, she became matron of a nurses school in Brussels, which is the capital of? - Yes! Belgium, and she was there when the First World War started in 1914.

Very soon her hospital was full of Belgian and German soldiers who had been wounded in the War, and it fell into German hands after they had captured Brussels. It was at this time that Nurse Cavell apart from her nursing, started a very dangerous job - she began to help escaped Allied soldiers to get over the frontier into the neighbouring country of Holland.

Well, as you can guess it did not take the Germans long to realise that these soldiers were somehow getting help and they became very suspicious of Edith and warned her of their suspicions.

Nurse Cavell took little notice of the German threats, and carried on helping Allied troops to escape across the border, until the Germans arrested her on 5th August 1915.

She was found guilty of treason and sentenced to death. Despite the protests from many countries, the Germans executed her by firing squad on 12th October 1915.

As you can imagine, the name of Edith Cavell became known throughout the world, and she became perhaps the greatest heroine in the nursing profession. Her story provides an example of both courage and loyal devotion to duty, and offers many lessons.

When the war reached her hospital, she could easily have left to a safe position but she choose to stay on even to work within enemy lines because she knew the sick and wounded needed her help.

As she helped troops to escape over the Dutch frontier, she knew she was breaking rules and risking herself, but her thoughts were on helping her country and those prisoners of war.

Many times in life, we run away from duty and from danger not because we are afraid of the danger - but because we are afraid of ourselves.

Nurse Cavell knowing that she faced death put her country and others first. When we are asked, or see a chance to help others, let us remember that brave nurse and if we act as she did, we shall all become heroes and heroines for God.

50. Strange Customs

In Sweden, as well as other Scandinavian countries, December 13th is quite an important day because it marks St. LUCIA'S Day, and there is an ancient and charming custom performed on that day.

Where there are several children in a family, the eldest daughter of the house dresses in white, and with candles forms in a ring or wreath round her head. Then she wakes the rest of the family in the morning with a breakfast of Lucia buns, which are bright yellow in colour and are made in several shapes and sizes.

Many other legends dating back to the Middle Ages are associated with St. Lucia's Day. To a Swedish housewife, Lucia Day is the day when all the Christmas baking and cleaning preparation must be completed. If it is, the legend says that St. Lucia will give the housewife prosperity and happiness all through the coming New Year.

Well, who was this St. Lucia or Lucy as she is sometimes called? It is said that she was from the island of Sicily off the coast of Italy, and it was there that she was put to death as a Christian martyr in the year 303 because of her faith.

There is little else known about this Saint except that it is thought she was named after the Roman goddess Lucina, who is said to be the patroness of newborn children helping them to first open their eyes and see the light of day.

It is thought that because of the name connection with the goddess Lucina, St Lucia is the patroness who guards against blindness or any other disease of the eyes, so if it is true, we have a lot to thank St. Lucia for, haven't we?

Perhaps on St. Lucia's Day on December 13th we might remember the gift of our eyes and sight, and those strange customs of Sweden. There is no need for you to make breakfast for the family or give them Lucia buns like the eldest daughter of a Swedish family, but we can in thankfulness for our sight - remember others who need our help.

It is with the thought for others, that we can remember too like the Swedish housewife, to get all our Christmas preparations done now. In two weeks time, we shall celebrate God's gift to the world in the birth of Jesus at Christmas, and you will all no doubt be receiving gifts and presents.

What is your gift to others going to be, particularly to the blind, the sick, and the poor? Now is the time for all of us to prepare, and may the story and customs of St. Lucia and her day help you to remember others.

51. A Christmas Post Office

Today, I want you to join me on a special Christmas magic-carpet journey - across the sea we go to Europe, over France and Germany until we see below us the snow covered mountains of Austria.

It is there in Upper Austria, not far from the town of STEYR, that we call on a tiny village called CHRISTKINDL, which in German means "Christ Child".

For eleven months of the year, it is a very quiet sleepy place like most other small villages. Even though it has a small Post Office, very few letters find their way there.

But when December draws near, it is a different story. Simply thousands and thousands of cards, letters, and parcels, begin to pile up at the tiny Post Office at Christkindl. If we called in at the Post Office today, we should see cards and letters coming from all over the world to be stamped with the "Christkindl" post mark before they are sent off again back to all parts of the globe.

In Austria, Father Christmas is almost unknown, because as many of you will know - each country has its own special form of Father Christmas; in some parts of Europe it is Saint Nicholas who brings the toys, and that is why to the Austrian children the Post Office at Christkindl means so much.

All their gifts and even their Christmas Tree, which are delivered on Christmas Eve are thought to be brought by the Christ Child Himself, and so a card or parcel with the stamp mark or postmark "Christkindl" has a very special meaning.

That is why all over the world, people each year send cards and letters and parcels (in another package) to "Postant, Christkindl, Austria," - to be stamped in this strange Christmas Post Office - "Christkindl" - from the Christ Child.

Once Christmas is over, the tiny village of Christkindl goes almost to sleep again, wrapped in a mantle of snow, to await another year before it springs into action again with its special Christmas Post Office.

Next week, when all our cards, and presents, and greetings, come to us - we might all remember that special little Post Office in the Austrian

Mountains, and in opening our presents say like the Austrian children, "Is it from Christkindl?" (Is it from the Christ child?) Because without Jesus, the Christ Child of Bethlehem - there would be no Christmas at all.

52. Christmas Stockings

Christmas is a time of many surprises particularly to boys and girls, and sometimes for grown-ups too, because we do not know who we are likely to get cards from, or what they will be like, or similarly with presents.

But Christmas also has its tradition with trees and carols, and hanging up one's stocking; have you ever wondered why children hang up stockings at Christmas to collect presents in? Well, I want to tell you today how the custom started.

As you know in this country we celebrate our Christmas Day on December 25th, but in parts of Europe Christmas is celebrated on December 15th, which is called the Feast of Saint Nicholas, for it is in these countries that St. Nicholas, like our Father Christmas, delivers the toys to the children.

Many years ago, in the town of MYRA, in Asia Minor, there lived a family of five, Mother, Father, and three sisters who were very poor. On the eve of St. Nicholas's Feast (their Christmas Day), they had no food in the house and no money, so St. Nicholas Day for them would be no Feast Day.

There was only one thing to do to save starving, and that was to go out begging, and so the parents, thinking that people may feel more sorry for the children, sent the three sisters out to beg.

Surely they would get at least some food for after all it was the eve of the great feast, and surely St. Nicholas would never see them starve. All evening they walked the streets of the town (so the legend tells us) for miles and miles they went knocking at doors and asking people in the street for money and food, but they did not get a single thing, and the rain began to fall.

Tired and wet, the three little sisters went home empty-handed and terribly disappointed. There was nothing to do but to go to bed and see what the following day would bring. Taking off their wet stockings, they hung them in front of the dying embers of the fire to dry for the morning, and off they went to bed.

But St. Nicholas had seen their plight. He saw them go out in faith to beg yet returned with nothing - he could not fail them on the eve of his

Feast Day. And so the story says, he climbed on the roof of their house and dropped three gold coins down the chimney - and what do you think happened?

Yes! The coins fell down the chimney stack and landed - one in each of the three sister's stockings which were hanging in front of the fire to dry.

In the morning, which was of course their Christmas Day, you can imagine the surprise the excitement when the three little girls came to put on their stockings, and how they were then able with the gold coins to buy food and presents.

Soon the news spread all round the town of what had happened and how kind St. Nicholas had been, and on the following years on the eve of St. Nicholas' Feast Day the boys and girls remembered the three sisters and hung up their stockings too at the base of the chimney stack so that St. Nicholas could drop presents for them down the chimney.

The custom soon spread all over Asia Minor, and soon to parts of Europe too - so that is why you hang up your stockings now on Christmas Eve.

Christmas is a time when Christians show their faith in believing in the birth of Jesus, and remember how God gave His Son for mankind, that is why we celebrate Christmas and give presents ourselves.

If you have faith, you will find that Father Christmas will not forget you and reward you for that faith - just like St. Nicholas did for the three little girls many years ago, so remember to hang up your stocking too.

53. The Silent Friend

Our story today is a true story about the sea. It was during the 1939 - 45 World War that the captain of a large liner had to make a journey across the Atlantic Ocean, which in war time meant that the voyage was full of danger because of enemy warships and submarines waiting to pounce on unprotected ships.

Before he sailed, the captain was given a secret code so that if he wanted help, he must send a wireless message in this secret code; he was also given a special route along which to sail and told to keep straight on this course and turn aside for nothing.

You can imagine that every day the captain and crew kept a sharp look-out for the enemy. All went well at first, but one day through the mist the captain saw the grey shape of ships.

He knew that there were no friendly or allied ships on this course, so he watched carefully through his binoculars, and finally because of their shape - he knew they were enemy cruisers.

By wireless he sent out a message for help and asking for instructions in the special code he had been given, and he was quite surprised at the message he received back, which when it was decoded said, "Keep straight on, I am standing by".

Well there were no other friendly ships in sight, but the captain knew that somewhere a friend was watching. And so the journey continued, the captain kept straight on this course and nothing happened, and he reached his English port safely.

A few hours after he had reached harbour, his ship was followed by a big British battleship, which had been standing by unseen - this was the silent friend.

If that ship in our story had left its course or path, it would probably have been seen and sunk by the enemy cruisers.

The captains orders were, "Keep straight on, I am standing by," so if we are advised to keep to a certain path or course in life, we too must obey orders and keep straight on.

It would have been so easy for that captain to have turned back, or to have taken another route away from the cruisers, but he knew that he must do as he had been told, and rely on his silent friend.

We too have silent friends watching over us, in the Bible we are told that we each have a guardian angel, who helps to keep us from harm. As we stand on the threshold of a New Year, let us remember that message to keep straight on. Remember that Jesus once said, "I will never leave you or forsake you".

So whatever dangers or perils we are in, we must keep straight on. He is standing by and will guard us and protect us, and finally lead us (like the captain and his ship) into a safe haven and through another year.